**Advance praise for *The Family Business Doctor***

"Dr. Fast has been a significant pioneer on family farm succession within Canadian Agriculture. His expertise and vast experience is reflected in *The Family Business Doctor*. He has provided training for many of us in the field and this book continues to be inspirational reading for all farmers and those of us who are professional advisors in the agricultural sector."

**Bob Ross, C-Team Co-ordinator, George Morris Centre, Guelph**

"Always an engaging and provocative speaker, our members gave Dr. Fast the highest marks for his presentations to our Family Business Forum. In *The Family Business Doctor*, John provides perceptive diagnosis and wise 'medicine' to help both generations of the family and the business to move together toward long-term health."

**Henry D. Landes, President, Delaware Valley Family Business Center, Pennsylvania**

"Dr. Fast has proved to be an invaluable facilitator and coach during a six-year succession planning process that has been demanding and sometimes even painful to our automobile group of companies employing ten family members. We have made great progress towards building a solid and effective program for the succession of our business that has been well-accepted by both the family participants and our staff. More importantly, our family relationships have emerged from this process with renewed strength and understanding. In *The Family Business Doctor*, John explores the full dynamics of business families and how to reach a successful transition to the next generation by providing readers with his vast experience and great sensitivity on this perplexing subject. I strongly recommend this book as required reading for the thousands of family business owners seeking guidance with managing their own business succession."

**Paul O'Regan, President,
O'Regan's Automotive Group, Halifax**

"*The Family Business Doctor* captures the accumulated wisdom of an advisor who respects and honours both family businesses and business families. The book reflects Dr. Fast's leadership within Canada in the understanding and integration of family dynamics into the succession planning process. I believe it also makes a significant contribution to the field because of its recognizable spiritual core. John has provided a key resource for business families and their advisors. It is well worth reading."

**John Bowey, Chairman, Deloitte & Touche LLP, Canada**

"A splendid book! Dr. Fast has captured the essence of what it means to be in a family business. His keen insights after years of research, personal business experience and listening to the poignant stories of those of us in business, make him an authority in helping family businesses to reach the next level of excellence. This book is a great resource for those looking for help."

**Herb Buller, Chairman, Norcraft Industries;**
**The Herb & Erna Buller Foundation, Winnipeg**

"John is able to zero in on the real issues surrounding business families. Not the challenges that seem to be urgent, but the ones that tug at our hearts and emotions and which we tend to bury unresolved, only to have them emerge later as a poisonous presence within the family. In following John's book and putting into action these methods of dealing with the deeper issues, we are able to move our working and family relationships to a higher, more rewarding level."

**Jim Hallman, CEO, Aberdeen Homes;**
**President, Hallman Construction, Kitchener-Waterloo**

"With *The Family Business Doctor*, John has, in his own robust and passionate way, provided an invaluable tool for family business members and their professional advisors. Having had the opportunity to work professionally with Dr. Fast on a number of matters as legal counsel, I understand and respect the key role that a person with his obvious expertise plays in ensuring that an appropriate family business succession plan can be successfully developed and implemented. This is definitely a text on the 'required reading' list."

**Douglas C. Jack, Solicitor, Fergus**

"Finally—a practical and sophisticated guide that addresses the 'head' and the 'heart' matters which commonly plague family business and compromise the health of the family and business. Dr. John Fast is a gifted specialist, and *The Family Business Doctor* reflects the many years of working with business families and their unique challenges. There is 'something for you' in this book, whether you are a family member or non–family member of a business family and you want to navigate through the issues to greater peace and greater successes."

**Cathy Keating, President, The Vault Jewellers, Halifax**

"I have known John for over ten years and have seen him work effectively with parents and children involved in their businesses. I have also seen him share his experience with other family business advisors through 'training the trainers' workshops. In this book John conveys the knowledge, skill and passion he has for families in business. Members of those families and their advisors will find it to be an enjoyable, enlightening and rewarding read."

**Jim Barnett, FCA, Director, School of Accountancy, University of Waterloo; Founding Board Member, Centre for Family Business**

# The
# FAMILY
# BUSINESS
## Doctor

### Ensuring the Long-Term Health of Your Business Family

John Fast, Ph.D.

Family Enterprise Solutions

www.familybusinessdoctor.ca

Library and Archives Canada Cataloguing in Publication

Fast, John G. (John George)
    The family business doctor : ensuring the long-term health of
your business family / John G. Fast.

Includes bibliographical references.
ISBN 978-0-9784490-0-1

    1. Family-owned business enterprises.  2. Family-owned business
enterprises--Succession.  3. Family-owned business enterprises--
Psychological aspects.  I. Title.

HD62.25.F38 2007             658'.045          C2007-905772-1

Printed in Canada

# Contents

# PREFACE

At times we all require the help of a physician. In this book the patient is the "business family"—the entire system of operational roles, legal agreements and emotional relationships that make up the complexity of modern family firms.

*The Family Business Doctor* provides a sophisticated diagnostic grid for the unique challenges faced by business families. But more importantly, this is a book about hope—charting healing pathways for the predictable aches and pains common to this patient.

For families facing succession, or stuck in sibling rivalry, or locked in chronic conflict patterns, to name but a few challenges, *The Family Business Doctor* shines a light on preventive solutions. The cures presented in this book are based on leading research, best practices and a decade of experience by Dr. John Fast in helping families navigate some of their deepest fears and operationalize their greatest desires.

Although it deals with practical issues like succession, this book is not a how-to primer. Rather, the following pages probe and deepen the individual capabilities and resources required to face constant change and transition. Each chapter addresses a unique theme and can be read as a stand-alone treatment. But together they provide a comprehensive guide to the soft issues inherent to business families. Reading, understanding and practising the "habits of the heart" articulated in the following pages will provide you with profound tools necessary for maintaining and strengthening what is most important to you—your business and your family.

# ACKNOWLEDGEMENTS

A book like this doesn't appear in a vacuum. The early encouragement and unwavering support of my friend Peter Hallman, coupled with his passion for family business, provided the initial impetus. In June of 1999 Peter and I were preparing to launch a training seminar on "SOBs: Sons of Bosses." Tragedy intervened, in the form of a fatal motorcycle accident. As a passionately engaged business and civic leader, Peter lived his life in order to make a difference. I trust that this book will honour Peter's legacy by continuing to make a difference for the many business family members who will be encouraged and supported through it.

James Barnett, author of *Transition Planning: An Advisor's Approach to Planning for the Business Owner* and director of the Master of Taxation program for the University of Waterloo School of Accountancy, was an early supporter in the establishment of the university's Centre For Family Business and has been a collaborator in developing a training program for professional advisors to family firms across Canada. Beyond his professional acumen in accounting, Jim's fly-fishing tips provided the necessary tonic of friendship as I navigated the waters of this new calling.

Henry Landes, president of the Delaware Valley Family Business Center in Pennsylvania, an early advisor, was very instrumental in helping me chart a strategic course through a new professional landscape.

Esther Falk Fast, my life partner for over thirty years, has been and continues to be the person who grounds me. As a clinical therapist and business partner, she and I have increasingly collaborated in assisting business families. She and our two daughters have taught me the most about what it means to be a circle of love.

A finished manuscript doesn't just magically appear out of nothing, and I have had very competent assistance in completing this book. Jennifer Martin was the capable and encouraging project manager who kept me on track and pulled together the various technical components that allowed this book to see the light of day. Rebecca Fast provided stellar copy-editing and creative assistance at crucial times during this project. Mark Bachmann provided the editorial and production oversight and served as a creative conversation partner.

Special credit and thanks goes to the hundreds of business families who invited me into their homes and into their hearts over the past decade. Although the themes are similar, each of you has a unique story. Many of your stories will be reflected in the following pages. Honouring confidentiality is of course essential in the building of a trusting relationship, and therefore the illustrative stories in this book are anonymous compilations of real situations faced by many business families. Whenever actual names are used, they are used with permission. This book attempts to honour what you hold most precious—both your family and your business.

# INTRODUCTION

## THE SUCCESSION CRISIS

The idea for this book had its origin in a series of workshops I conducted in southwestern Ontario during the mid-1990s. In my dual role at that time as president of a major financial institution and faculty member of Conrad Grebel College at the University of Waterloo, I was attempting to increase the level of conversation between a region rich with vibrant businesses and a value-based community of meaning with its unique historical and intellectual heritage. In some ways these workshops were another stab at narrowing the "town-gown" divide. However, there were three elements that made them unique and memorable.

The first novelty was that the entire series of workshops had the sponsorship of three diverse institutions: a financial institution, a university/college, and a religious denomination. Secondly, although I had written my Ph.D. dissertation on "business ethics" and taught at universities in California and Boston, I chose not to go to my files and pull out favourite lecture topics. Instead, I drew on my entrepreneurial background, which began at the age of twenty and continued with the founding, managing and selling of a small chain of bookstores in New England. It seemed that my involvement guaranteed that the voices of the business community would be genuinely heard and honoured. Thirdly, and perhaps most importantly, I had the support and encouragement of a significant number of business leaders. They graciously served as an exploratory focus group, allowing the entire learning experience to remain current and relevant.

> ## *"These were some of the best two hours spent in my life."*

The above comment by a local business leader came after a particularly memorable evening focused on the topic of "family business succession." By an overwhelming margin, the biggest issue facing this particular business community in southwestern Ontario could be summarized as *family business dynamics*, with the focus on succession planning. I can't count the number of times business owners asked me, "John, can you help us? How do we pass our businesses on to our children? How do we handle our kids in the business?" Unknowingly, I had tapped into a huge demographic phenomenon: the leading edge of a baby boom generation of owner-operators facing retirement while involved in business with adult children. Voluntary and involuntary changes were looming on the horizon on both business and personal levels for these family firms. Confusion reigned. The net result was a dangerously low level of planning for the future.

My own response to this identified need and subsequent request for help was both very personal and immediate. I listened to friends who were running family firms—to their dreams, their pain, their confusion, successes and failures. Their stories were compelling. And as they kept coming back for advice, it became clear that they weren't just asking for help in managing and growing their businesses.

They needed more focused and intensive help in order to successfully negotiate their delicate family dynamics while managing their own lives. Certain questions kept reoccurring. Why won't my father listen to me? How can we give honest criticism to our kids?

How can I let go of a previous betrayal? How am I going to be fair to all my children? Why doesn't the family appreciate all my hard work? How can I get out of this trapped situation?

I began to hear common themes. Betrayal, lack of trust, inadequate and dysfunctional communication patterns, wildly divergent intergenerational expectations and assumptions, unresolved conflict and closely guarded family secrets were dominant among them. There was an overall sense that these families were stuck and scared of losing whatever semblance of a family they had, and they felt utterly alone. Most business families thought that their issues were entirely unique to themselves and had no idea where to go for help. It was this sense of aloneness, echoed in so many family businesses, that prompted my response.

They needed help and I attempted to provide it. Having spent seventeen years of my professional life in the United States, I was aware of the over one hundred university-based family business institutes that were attempting to educate business families. In fact, one of the first of these institutions began at Goshen College in Indiana, a Mennonite sister institution to Conrad Grebel College. Its founding director, Len Geiser, provided me with important early assistance. In Canada, CAFE (Canadian Association of Family Enterprise) had chapters in a number of major cities that provided a loose support and networking umbrella for family firms. However, at that time there was nothing within easy reach of southwestern and central Ontario. In 1997, together with a key group of fifteen founding family firms and the inspirational leadership of the late Peter Hallman, a prominent business leader in the Waterloo region, we created the Centre for Family Business, affiliated with the University of Waterloo. Within five years of its inception, membership had grown to over sixty business families. Today the Centre continues to provide a vibrant and supportive program serving family businesses across southern Ontario. I believe that the success of the Centre, considered one of the largest membership-based family business centres in North America, comes from the clarity of purpose conceived by its founding members. Business families articulated this purpose very clearly: "We need a safe place where we can talk about our unique issues." They mandated that approximately 80% of programming should involve education on "soft issues." By this they meant the behavioural, relational and family dynamics components of owning and managing family firms.

I had the privilege of serving as the founding executive director of the Centre for Family Business for seven years. During a sabbatical in 1998, I formally launched my own consulting and training company, Family Enterprise Solutions, and resigned from my university positions. But more importantly, I had stumbled upon a calling. I use "calling" advisedly, for the term conjures up qualities such as passion and purpose and meaning. I had discovered an arena that was complex enough to fully challenge my range of skills and training; that was intrinsically motivating, in that success was measured in changed lives and behaviour; and that brought together the two aspects of my own personal and professional life, namely the entrepreneurial and the academic. The word "calling" also carries with it a spiritual connotation, which remains a key ingredient in my ongoing work with business families. My approach with all my clients is one of intrinsic respect and honour for the divine spark that resides in each of us, a sense that we are all created for a purpose that ultimately transcends profit, and a conviction that miracles are possible—no matter how difficult the situation or bitter the conflict. Most importantly, I believe it is a sense of caring and hope projected into the many complex and acute crisis situations that business families face that has made the greatest difference. That legacy continues to be measured by successful business transitions, strengthened family relationships and individual lives lived with greater meaning and purpose.

The writing of this book is a response to the many requests I have received from clients and family business audiences who continue to ask for a distillation of the themes and insights shared when we gather together as fellow-learners. Although this is not a how-to book, I believe that understanding the "best practices," or what I enumerate as "successful habits," is a vital first step in developing action plans that actually work. I have encountered too many clients who have spent tens of thousands of dollars on grand schemes to minimize taxes, only to belatedly discover that the technical succession scenario laid out doesn't meet the actual needs and goals of the family or its individual members. I trust that there are enough nuggets and practical tips throughout these chapters for you to dive in and either start or continue to work with your family in charting a future for your business that is both profitable and personally empowering.

# SECTION I

## FAMILY BUSINESSES ARE UNIQUE

# CHAPTER 1:

# THE COMPETITIVE ADVANTAGES OF FAMILY FIRMS

*"Family-run businesses generally outperform*
*non-family companies."*

In the early 1990s, *Inc.* magazine editorialized that "it might not be easier to run a business with family members. But when family businesses work, they possess an inborn competitive advantage no other company can match."[1] This sentiment contrasts with popular notions that family firms are fraught with difficult and seemingly intractable issues. Often cited are founders who run their family businesses as private fiefdoms. Another favourite stereotype is next-generation members, cynically referred to as "the lucky sperm club,"[2] who ruin the family fortune within three generations. But Adam Bellow, in his recent book *In Praise of Nepotism*, leads the charge in arguing on behalf of the advantages of kinship in business. He contends that "nepotism works, it feels good, and it is generally the right thing to do."[3] An impressive amount of supporting evidence seems to bolster his claim that family-run businesses generally outperform non-family companies.

The front cover of the November 10, 2003 issue of *BusinessWeek* reads "Surprise! One third of the S&P 500 companies have founding families involved in management. And those are usually the best performers." In fact, according to this special issue on family business, their performance far outstripped that of non-family companies. The issue indicated that annual shareholder return for family companies averaged 15.6%, compared to 11.2% for non-family companies. Return on assets averaged 5.4% per year for the family group vs. 4.1% for non-family companies. And the family firms trumped the others on annual revenue growth (23.4% to 10.8%) and income growth (21.1% to 12.6%).[4] In the June 2003 issue of the *Journal of Finance*, Ronald C. Anderson and David M. Reeb presented research on the performance of S&P 500 Index stocks that clearly contradicted "anecdotal accounts and prior literature suggesting that continued founding-family ownership in U.S. corporations is an organizational form that leads to poor performance."[5]

Smart investors have been analyzing the numbers and many are switching to family firms. Particularly now, when trust in senior management has declined in the wake of recent corporate scandals, family-controlled companies have become more attractive to investors. A recent study by Philippe Tibi at UBS shows that share prices of France's top seventeen family-controlled public companies have risen an average of 146% since 1993, compared to just 48% for France's CAC-40 index as a whole. Tibi says, "This group (family companies) has been outperforming to such a shocking extent it makes you raise your eyebrows and want to look for an explanation" (*Financial Times*, October 25, 2003).[6]

There are good explanations. What are the secret competitive advantages of family firms? Recent studies point to a focus on investing for the long term, a reluctance to manipulate current earnings, and the fact that family ownership "mitigates managerial opportunism." The *BusinessWeek* special issue identifies six key advantages:

1. Family firms create a culture of leadership opportunity and mentoring.
2. Family corporations can make quicker decisions because there is usually no gap between senior management and owners.

3. Family companies breed loyalty, which leads to reduced turn-over and higher productivity.
4. Founders and their offspring tend to reinvest heavily in their businesses, which results in patient capital.
5. Family business boards don't act like absentee landlords. The research showed that "large personal and financial stakes in the company's future give family directors a powerful incentive to hold management accountable—and the clout with which to do so."
6. The Legacy Factor seems to imbue family managers with a sense of deeper commitment, something that "stock options and eight-figure salaries just can't buy."

So why have current business programs been so slow to examine family firms and teach their management practices as models of accomplishment? Adam Hanft, in a September 2003 *Inc.* magazine article, writes that family firms remain ghettoized by business academics: "We've been trained that businesses are machines, agnostic to personality and passion. If that were the case, family-run businesses wouldn't outperform those run by the M.B.A./executive recruiter axis."[7]

The greatest competitive advantage of family firms, namely, trust, is best understood when family companies are compared to public firms. The trust between investors who buy stock in a public company and that company's management is a major contributor to overall investor confidence in the stock market. Continued revelations of public company financial miscues and allegations of deception have sorely taxed that essential commodity of trust. And we have all seen the results in the subsequent declining market.

After all, the job of top executives in most public companies is unequivocal and straightforward: "Increase shareholder value." This is the reason these executives receive their large paycheques, and their success or failure is measured by the stock market every business day. The inexorable pressure to increase shareholder value leads many to present the appearance of success even when the reality is something else.

According to the *Wall Street Journal*, a "1998 survey found two-thirds of financial executives complaining of pressures from upstairs to make the numbers look better by dubious means." Another study detailing accounting scandals found that fraud started at the top in over 70% of the cases examined. And the litany of large public companies recently indicted, convicted or accused of misrepresentation continues to grow (Nortel, Enron, WorldCom, Vivendi, Martha Stewart—to name just a few in the last several years). Apparently, the goal of many chief executives has been to create for investors an illusion of value that did not match reality. In doing so they defrauded the one constituency they claim to serve, according to the only criterion recognized as legitimate by the marketplace—namely, shareholder value.

Family business owners tend to view "shareholder value" differently. Instead of high stock prices, real, lasting values tend to be the family business goal. Shares in a family business cannot be easily disposed of by casually placing a phone call.

Indeed, the whole notion of shareholder value is rarely discussed in family businesses. In terms of the attention it receives, most family business owners treat it more like an accounting footnote than as a constant ticker on a computer screen. Instead, the hourly realities of clients, employees and suppliers are their primary concerns. They focus on the people within the larger community of their business family who make it possible and profitable to remain in business every day. Because of their dependence on the goodwill of these constituencies, family business owners carefully balance the interests of these groups with their own interests in order to build long-term value.

The deterioration of trust in the current stock markets again highlights the greatest competitive advantage of family businesses—trust. Family business owners reside in and act as contributing members of their communities. Their actions are an open book to their community, and therefore family business owners must reinforce trust continually on many levels: with other family members, with customers who belong to the same branch of the Rotary Club, with employees who attend the same church, with suppliers and other key long-term business relationships. Family firms that treat business merely as a financial game with rules meant to be broken do not last.

The most successful family businesses that I have known and worked with have built real, lasting and value-based trust within their families and in their commercial relationships. Their values are the values that are essential to the development of any humane and civil society. Their success is defined not only by wealth created, but also by the fulfillment experienced by family members and by the health of their community. Ultimately, these family business owners are deeply committed to becoming good stewards of their private enterprises. Perhaps that is why they rarely discuss shareholder value.

# CHAPTER 2

## THE FOUR UNIQUE CHALLENGES
## FACING BUSINESS FAMILIES

*"Entrepreneurs are great at entrance strategies. After
all, they've created companies, often from scratch.
Their weakness is exit strategies."*[1]

The absence of timely succession planning can sometimes be attributed to the dearth of relational capital within the business family. Someone once quipped, "Men are more concerned with net worth than with family worth." Whether that generalization is true or not, we know that the rugged individualism and the driving entrepreneurial abilities of the founding generation—to gut out the hard times, work long hours and keep their cards close to their chests—often work against the more collaborative process required to help the family through a business succession process. Many founders haven't accumulated much relational goodwill in the family bank account. And, since the succession process is mainly about open and honest communication, it requires all of the emotional elasticity that a family can muster.

Family firms provide much of the world's entrepreneurial energy. In developing countries it is estimated that 98% of all economic activity is driven by business families. Estimates in North America indicate that from 50% to 70% of the total economy is made up of family firms, depending on the measuring stick used

(GDP or total number of employees). In some industry sectors, agriculture being one example, family businesses make up 99% of all business activity. Family business is big business. Most major financial institutions have recognized this fact by attempting to understand business families more comprehensively and then devising effective strategies to better serve this market. It has escaped no one's notice that over one trillion dollars worth of assets are about

> ## *"Family business is big business."*

to change generational hands in the next ten years; most of that wealth resides in family-owned and operated companies.

In my work I have found that the unique challenges facing family firms seem to crystallize around the dilemma of succession. For business families, the word "succession" often represents a very complex constellation of assumptions, expectations, plans and emotions that are well nigh indecipherable. The reality is that "succession" is actually another word for change—a sort of change that reaches into almost every crevice of a business family's life. Since most of us are hard-wired to fear change, is it any wonder that succession planning receives such belated and cursory attention?

A significant gender difference exists on the issue of transitions. Women tend to view change as an opportunity for growth, whereas men tend to view change as a loss. This divergence increases as people age and helps to explain why in many family companies it is often the women behind the scenes who drive whatever succession planning process exists.

The unique challenges facing family enterprises can be described more clearly and accurately by comparing the results of three recent national surveys of family firms: the *American Family Business Survey* (2003), conducted by MassMutual Financial Group and the Raymond Institute;[2] *Are Canadian Family Businesses an Endangered Species? The First Success Readiness Survey of Canadian Family-Owned*

*Business* (1999), conducted by Deloitte & Touche;[3] and lastly, the 2003 *BDO Dunwoody/Compas Report on Canadian Family Business.*[4]

To begin with, these surveys identified the massive changes about to overtake family business leadership in North America. Over half of the current leaders of Canadian family firms planned to retire within ten years, and three-quarters within fifteen years, according to the Deloitte & Touche study. The MassMutual survey showed that 39% of U.S. family-owned businesses would undergo a change of leadership within the next five years, and 56% within ten years. This imminent and unprecedented turnover will entail four challenges that are unique to family-owned and operated companies.

### *Strategic Business Challenge*

It is an axiom in business that you get what you measure, and measuring usually requires a strategic planning process and a written plan. However, in the MassMutual survey only 37% of respondents reported having a written strategic business plan. The Deloitte & Touche survey found it disturbing that only 40% of Canadian family businesses had a business plan and less than 25% had a long-term strategic plan. For many of these owners the strategic plan is in their head, and as long as it remains only there it becomes difficult to operationalize succession.

Although these leaders may not be consciously aware of it, their inability or refusal to do more serious planning is actually a fearful default stance that tells the rest of the family and their employees that "I am afraid of change and of losing control; therefore let's not interrogate future reality too seriously." And since many of these founders do not have a formal accountability structure such as an independent board, they can usually proceed with impunity. This often means that little or no planning is done.

As the surveys noted and as can be seen from the title *Are Canadian Family Businesses an Endangered Species?*, such a stance is a recipe for business disaster. The lack of strategic business planning carries over into other areas of planning. According to the Deloitte & Touche survey, fewer than 40% of family firms have contingency plans in place in case of unforeseen death or disability. And over 63% do not know what their tax liability to the estate would be if both owners/spouses were to die today. In the area of succession, 66% of Canadian family firms have not even established a process for selecting a successor. In the U.S., of the family business CEOs expected to retire within five years, 42% have not chosen a successor.

In my consulting experience I have found some industry sectors, agriculture being a notable example, in which these statistics are actually much worse. The fundamental issue is one of transferring power and control in a meaningful and timely manner. And the deeper question for family business owners is really, "What are you afraid of?"

## The Challenge of Balancing Family and Business

Despite the considerable competitive advantages of families working together in the same business, many of these families struggle with how best to maintain a healthy balance between family and business concerns. The BDO Dunwoody/Compas family business portrait coined the term "family-preneurs" to describe individuals in this group and discovered that their biggest problem was an inability to go home to relax. It was difficult to establish effective boundaries between family life and business activities.

According to the survey, entrepreneurial families rarely had explicit rules to live by. Only 11% claimed to have written guidelines governing family obligations, and 24% talked about a set of unwritten rules. Perhaps the absence of written guidelines reflects the general lack of planning of these families. A more probable explanation is the tendency in many family cultures to function on the assumption that members can read each other's minds. Although this pattern may have worked in more traditional, authoritarian and/or rural cultures where the mind of the elder (usually father) was the mind that ruled, modern democratic families with adult children are a more unruly lot to manage, let alone integrate into a business system.

The challenge of establishing good communication between business and family systems—perhaps the most common and chronic problem of all family businesses—can be gleaned between the lines of the various surveys. The Deloitte & Touche study describes this difficulty of "listening." "With respect to considering the personal goals of family members, 48% indicated that personal goals of family members working in the business were considered, while only 29% considered personal goals of family members not working in the business" (p. 13). Based on my experience working with family firms, even these numbers seem optimistic. For a clearer picture, one would need to ask what the survey participants meant by "considered." Does "considered" mean that individual family members were allowed to see a draft plan in order to rubber stamp it? Or does "considered" mean that individuals in the family felt safe enough to vigorously engage other family members in a process that debated honest differences of opinion?

Of course, this raises an even more basic strategic question: when is it appropriate to consider individual family members' goals and opinions in the ongoing management of the business? The confusion resulting from this complex balancing act is the cause of over 50% of the difficulties that all business families face.

### The Challenge of the Vulnerable Next Generation

Generally accepted worldwide succession statistics for family firms have put the success rate for transferring a business to the second generation at 30%; to the third, at 15%; and to the fourth generation, at 5%. This does not mean that selling the family business to an outside party is necessarily a preferred exit strategy. However, these statistics indicate just how difficult intergenerational successions can be. Yet the majority of family firms continue to view such a succession strategy as desirable. (Although there is a considerable difference between U.S. and Canadian family firms on this point. Nearly 88% of U.S. family enterprises desire to remain family-owned and controlled. In Canada, keeping the business in the family was viewed as "not important" by 43% of businesses surveyed. In fact, 43% of Canadian business families indicated that they were planning to sell the business.)

Some additional national differences emerge from these surveys. Most of the U.S. family businesses represented in the MassMutual survey started shortly after World War II, whereas two-thirds of the family-owned businesses in the Deloitte & Touche Canadian survey were founded after 1970. The majority (77%) of Canadian firms valued their operations at up to $5 million, whereas the mean annual revenue of the U.S. firms was $36.5 million. Although there are clear differences among the groups surveyed, overall significant numbers of family businesses have the desire (some might view it as a fantasy) to keep the business in the family.

However, the lack of preparation and planning being done to fulfill this dream leaves the next generation vulnerable. Of those Canadian owners who think it is important to retain family ownership, "41% have children involved in ownership and 31% plan to have their children involved in ownership before the parents retire. However, only 7% have transferred control to the next generation, while 39% plan to do it before they retire and 17% expect to do it on retirement" (Deloitte & Touche, p. 11).

In the MassMutual survey close to 14% of CEOs said they would "never" retire—a signal indicating the rigidity of many family business leaders and the resultant transition difficulties. This seeming lack of next-generation preparation and general lack of succession planning, coupled with the fact that only 41% of leaders surveyed indicated that they frequently discussed business issues with their children (20% said they did so seldom or never), leaves members of the next generation in something of a quandary. Their profound sense of vulnerability begins subtly and crescendoes into later adulthood. Many have families of their own and want to plan for the future of these families. However, if they work for their parents without a clear succession plan, they are often unable to get on with their own family planning. This can lead to frustrating feelings of being trapped, and the resulting sense of disempowerment spills over into many other areas of their lives.

Inadequate planning for the future by the senior generation puts the next generation at risk. The MassMutual survey indicated that more than a third of the next-generation respondents had

> **"Fourteen percent of CEOs said they would 'never' retire—a signal indicating the rigidity of many family business leaders and the resultant transition difficulties."**

no knowledge of the senior generation's share-transfer intentions. And although senior family members cited concerns about management strength as one of their greatest challenges and generally expressed the belief that their children would someday own and operate their businesses, next-generation leadership selection and development by senior family members was notably absent.

The root of the vulnerability felt by next-generation members can be found in the deep emotional tension between loyalty to the family of origin, which often includes the family business, and an individual sense of purpose and self-determination. These creative tensions exist in most families, but within the more complex overlay of working for the family company these emotions can and do frequently erupt into chronic, deep-seated and personally destructive conflict.

### The Difficulty with the Succession Planning Process
There are a number of key reasons why business families find it so difficult even to start the succession planning process. Some families believe that succession means a quick fix, taking a magic pill or

implementing a straightforward tax strategy from their accountant. When they realize that transferring the family business to the next generation is not just one simple act but a process that may take years to complete, many are afraid to begin. It is estimated that the average succession planning process takes two to five years of rigorous emotional engagement and some fairly hard-nosed negotiating. Such a prolonged period of intense intergenerational contact increases the potential for friction between parents and successors and between members of the family who are working in the business and those who are not.

Succession planning and retirement are often linked together. The two generations have polarized emotional responses to the inevitable life-stage transition that is called retirement. As a result, family members often mean very different things when using the same words. To the older generation, retirement might simply mean a reduction in management responsibilities. To the next generation, a parent's retirement might be understood as an opportunity: "Finally I get the chance to manage the business my way." The entire succession planning process, which is a direct result of contemplating some sort of retirement redirection, is often viewed uneasily by company founders who see it as the first nail in their coffin, whereas members of the younger generation tend to embrace it and feel relief when the process is settled and they can make firm plans for the future. Therefore it should come as no surprise if succession planning is done infrequently or in a slipshod manner.

The stubbornness and pride of the older generation can also prevent the seeking of outside expertise during this time. Unfortunately, autocratic control can be a cover-up for the insecurity and fear that inhibit the transparent communication necessary for the family to manage the complex emotional issues involved in any succession process.

# CHAPTER 3

## THE PRIORITY OF A COMMON FAMILY VISION

S tarting any succession process with an articulated common vision has a number of benefits:

1. A common vision helps *unite* the family around a goal that is larger than the family and bigger than individual greed and competition.
2. A common vision functions to *inspire* the family during the difficult times and motivates family members to sacrifice for the common good of the family.
3. A common vision provides the family with a set of core principles and guidelines with which to *evaluate* family and individual behaviour. This is particularly useful when there is a problematic family member.
4. A common vision *informs* the individual growth and development of the next generation.
5. A common vision (if it is revisited and revised regularly) *provides a change model* for both individual growth and business development.

Achieving unity and attempting to keep together what the family business leaders have spent a lifetime creating involves broadening the definition of success. Harnessing the inborn competitive advantage of close partnerships that often function like extended families requires paying more attention to the stewardship of values and the equity embodied within their relational capital. Keeping stakeholders connected within a web of significant meaning involves the transfer not only of money and assets, but also of psychic energy.

How is that done well? The first step is to address the core concerns and ask a series of foundational questions. Who am I as an individual? What defines us as a family? Do we share common val-

> **"It has been estimated that 80% of business family failures are the result of unresolved and destructive family dynamics."**

ues? Do we have common goals? Family businesses that succeed in the long term have developed the habit of asking these questions in creative ways and have found methods for harnessing the power of a common vision for themselves. Families that are afraid to ask these questions and do not want to articulate and record their common vision, or families that, after engaging in such an exercise, discover that they really don't have a common vision, will have difficulty in retaining the business within the family.

When I began consulting with family firms I often made the mistake of leaving this step until the end of the succession planning process. I belatedly realized that the entire process could be enhanced and accelerated once the family members found a way to articulate their common vision and goals. If they were unable to find unity of purpose—and this would usually become painfully obvious—they could spare themselves the expenditure of energy and resources needed to engage in a succession planning process that was usually doomed to failure. It has been estimated that 80% of business family failures are the result of unresolved and destructive family dynamics. Therefore developing and defining a common vision or understanding of success is the essential first step in succession planning and in enhancing business family harmony.

### Defining Success

There are numerous ways to measure success in a family business. Healthy earnings, strong shareholder equity growth, systematic wealth retention and a completed family ownership transfer could be part of the definition. Because it is assumed that a prosperous family business is good for its owners, employees, customers and community (and the related accountants, attorneys, financial planners, etc.), no effort is spared in seeking to improve business performance according to these measures.

However, I would suggest a broader understanding of success. The definition of success for a family business must include relational criteria that reflect the larger health of the family and its individual members. Thus a healthy family business transition would include the following characteristics:

- The next generation has the opportunity to make a significant contribution to the business.
- Intergenerational decision-making is occurring.
- The next generation has the opportunity to engage in personally rewarding work.
- The transition process does not result in any serious personal casualties.

When the above criteria are lacking, the ongoing operation of a family business might actually perpetuate existing family problems. In such cases the family business can function to impede the normal development of the family members, particularly those belonging to the next generation. This can result in increasing emotional pain for individual family members, chronic conflict, splintered families and stagnant businesses.

### Defining Family

So what is a family? Families are technically defined as persons connected by blood. But I would like to broaden the definition and proffer the following as an expression of what many of us might desire, although we sometimes find it difficult to define and practise:

> **"We all want our families to be 'circles of love,' caring, mutually supportive relationships which help each member to thrive."**

Building such healthy families is not easy. In his book *The Seven Habits of Healthy Families*, Stephen Covey writes that "good families, even great families, are off track 90% of the time. The key is that they have a sense of destination."[1] What does this destination look like? And is this destination of family health a shared one? Therefore the first question for families in business should be, "Do we have a clear sense of what we want our "circle of love" to look like?" F. Walsh, writing in the *Family Business Review*, presents the following summary of characteristics that can help families open the discussion:[2]

- The members of our family care deeply for each other and we are a mutually supportive relationship unit.
- Our family respects individual differences, autonomy and separate needs. We foster the development and well-being of members in each generation.
- For couples, our relationships are between equal partners, characterized by mutual respect, support and sharing of power, privilege and responsibilities.
- Our family exercises effective parental leadership and authority to nurture and protect children and take care of the elderly and other vulnerable family members. Our family has adequate re-

sources for basic economic security and for emotional support in our extended family and friendship networks.

- Our family is stable. Our patterns of interaction are characterized by clarity, consistency and predictability.
- Our family has enough flexibility to cope effectively with stress and the problems and challenges that come with the changes and transitions throughout the life cycle.
- Our family has open communication that is characterized by clarity of rules and expectations, pleasurable interaction and a wide range of emotional expression and empathic responses.
- Our family has effective problem-solving and conflict-resolution processes. We share a belief system that enhances mutual trust, problem mastery and connectedness with past and future generations and fosters core values and a concern for the larger human family.

Building a healthy family requires at least some level of agreement as to what constitutes "health." Assessing how the family is actually functioning in the areas identified is another matter entirely. But the business families that are successful over time find a way to honestly diagnose their own health according to an agreed-upon grid of definitions and expectations.

### Defining a Family Vision

Defining a family vision is important for any business family. Successful family businesses often address this foundational strategy by writing out a family mission statement. Why is such a statement so crucial? According to Stephen Covey, "many families are managed on the basis of crisis, moods, quick fixes and instant gratification—not on sound principles. Symptoms surface whenever stress and pressure mount. The core of any family is what is changeless, what is always going to be there—shared vision and values. By writing a family mission statement, you give expression to its true foundation. This mission statement becomes its constitution, the standard, the criterion for evaluation and decision-making. It gives continuity and unity to the family as well as direction."[3]

A common destination is the result of shared family values, a common culture and regular communication. However, most business families do not take the time to explore and articulate their core values. Their reluctance may be due in part to the potential for conflict between personal values and the values of the business. In most areas those values may be complementary; however, the personal value of a "balanced life" might conflict with the business value of "hard work."

Intergenerational differences often surface over differing understandings of concepts like "respect," "power," "security," "belonging," "achievement" and "advancement." These different understandings are completely normal in all families and family firms. The difficulty lies in learning to communicate with each other around those differences and around the mutually shared values of listening, tolerance, honesty and recognition in spite of differences. Too many families violate core values such as self-control, intimacy and friendship because they cannot honestly discuss nuanced differences on other values. Or sometimes the values articulated and displayed in the business seem to conflict with what is being taught in the home.

In my work I have found it helpful to encourage families to write out a core vision. For families that are religiously inclined, a prayer can function as a way of expressing this core vision. Frequently I encourage such families to write their own "family prayer" and sometimes I introduce them to the following litany:

### *Prayer for Loving-Kindness*
*May our family be filled with loving-kindness.*
*May our family be well.*
*May our family be peaceful and at ease.*
*May our family be happy.*

An example of a family mission statement:

> *Our family strives to live a balanced life centred on the giving and receiving of mutual support and affection. Through all our activities we will attempt to empower our family, friends, employees and our extended communities with hope. We want to use our individual and family gifts and talents to their fullest potential as we seek to make a difference in our world.*

> **"Plans are useless—planning is everything."**
> **– Eisenhower**

### How to Formulate a Family Vision

It's the planning process that really matters. Perhaps I can add that visions written down on paper do provide the family with a certain discipline, but more importantly they provide the family with an opportunity to openly share and discuss those values, goals and dreams that are too often left unspoken or misinterpreted. Three very simple questions can help family members identify those individual goals and dreams so that they can begin fashioning an ideal family vision.

The first question: *In your ideal vision for your family business, what are the family values that you want to see practised?*

Another way of asking this question is to identify the core, life-giving forces that enable your family to make it through hard times. The process of communicating regularly with each other results in a common culture of shared family values. As family members identify their three to five most important values in both personal and business arenas, further discussion can clarify the areas in which they are complementary and those in which individual family members see a potential for conflict. For example, personal values such as security and peace might be juxtaposed against business values such as prosperity and achievement. Individuals within a family might also have different understandings of values such as health and fairness and power.

The second question begins to personalize the vision: *In your ideal vision for your family business, what specific talents or gifts are you sharing within your family business?*

Perhaps family members can share an incident or occasion when they felt especially excited about being part of the family. In recalling and sharing these peak experiences (or lack of them), they will soon discover "what really matters." This question begins to explore feelings of self-worth and perceived competence as they relate to actual events for individuals within the family system.

The third question functions as a barometer of general family health because the answers will reflect the degree to which the ideal vision is being actualized: *In your ideal vision for your family business, how are you being acknowledged or appreciated for your efforts so that you feel valued?*

Every family member comes to every interaction with three core questions reverberating in the back of his or her mind: Am I worthy? Am I competent? Can I influence events in my life? How other family members respond to them in expressing acknowledgement and appreciation will influence their answers to these three core questions. How individuals handle the response—their perceptions and feelings—matters. The whole point of this discussion is to create a climate in which family members will feel well-treated and, when they feel differently, will be able to safely ask questions, seek more detailed feedback and continue learning.

Genuinely supportive family business environments are difficult to implement because of the inherent clash of core values between the competitive world of business and the idealized world of family harmony—but the effort to do so can yield big dividends.

## Assessing Your Family Vision:
## How Does Your Family Function?

1. Do we spend time together as a family?
2. Do we talk and listen to each other frequently?
3. Do we respect differences and encourage interests outside the family?
4. Do we communicate directly and honestly and avoid gossip?
5. Can we handle conflict in direct, non-hurtful ways?
6. How frequently do we express appreciation for each other and demonstrate that we care?
7. Can we have fun together as a family?
8. Even when we disagree, is there respect and good-will among family members?
9. Is the loyalty between next-generation couples as strong as or stronger than that between parents and children?
10. Do we share a common vision?

# CHAPTER 4

## THREE BOTTOM LINES:
## LOVE, MONEY, POWER

Business families face a degree of complexity that ordinary families and other businesses just don't have to face. Their lack of awareness about, and inability to manage, intersecting roles often results in much confusion. It is estimated that more than half of all business conflict would be avoided or minimized if the family business stakeholders could differentiate these roles and stop confusing them.

The difficulty in family businesses is that family members are required to wear three different hats almost simultaneously. At any given moment of the day they could be assuming the role of father/mother/son/daughter; the role of boss or employee; and the role of shareholder or owner. Many of us do not recognize the significant differences that these various roles entail. Even when we understand, many of us find it extremely difficult to separate the requirements and expectations of these roles. Healthy and successful business families find creative ways of keeping business agendas and family roles distinct and separate.

I want to share a classic story highlighting the problematic youngest son—let's call him Skip—of a successful farm operation. Skip, who at twenty-six was a spoiled and entitled member of a family business that employed two other children as well, had the tendency to arrive late for work and leave early in the day for personal errands. While at work, concentration and productivity were not his strong suits. On one occasion he mixed some bad feed, causing the loss of a significant number of livestock. When this happened a second time, the accountant counselled the business owner (Skip's dad) to deal aggressively with the situation. But Dad was not allowed to fire Skip because Skip's mother intervened, asking her husband to "give him another chance." Within a few months, and after another significant loss of livestock due to negligence with feed production, the family's banker weighed in with grave concern. The owner felt he had no choice. In an awkward encounter in his office, he fired Skip. Then he got up slowly from behind his desk, put his arm around Skip, and said, "Now son, as your dad, how can I help you find a new job?"

This story illustrates the difficulty of keeping our roles distinct. How many of us can be an effective boss and a good father at the same time? How many of us can be a good mom and a boss? Or, how many of us can function as a caring brother and a supervisor simultaneously? One of the more difficult situations I have recently encountered was a husband who had lost confidence in his wife's accounting capabilities but couldn't engage in an honest discussion with her about the matter, much to the detriment of their rather extensive business. Keeping the integrity of a role in one sphere of activity from diminishing the effectiveness of a role in another arena is well-nigh impossible. One of the keys to healthy interpersonal family dynamics is to more fully understand the three distinct roles within family firms. We will do so by examining their unique mandates.

### The Family Circle

The bottom line in a healthy family is love and the maintaining of harmonious relationships. We all want our families to be circles of love—caring, mutually supportive relationships that help each member to thrive. But maintaining good relationships can be a difficult day-to-day grind. Success entails a deep concern for a common history, shared traditions and the passing on of core values to the next generation. The family is the place where most of us first experience strong passion, and it is the place where we develop the capacity for loyalty. The family is the arena of life-long commitments. It is in the family that members continue to expect almost unconditional acceptance. Loyalty and trust represent the currency that is traded in the bank of relational capital. Children expect

> **"The family is where we learn what attributes are essential to our relations with future partners, be they intimate partners or business partners."**

to receive nurturing, young adults expect affirmation and adults expect mutual respect. These are the bottom-line expectations for most family members. The family is where we learn what attributes are essential to our relations with future partners, be they intimate partners or business partners.

How do families accomplish the task of broadening and deepening their "circle of love?" Healthy families build relational capital by, firstly, nurturing the healthy development of individual members throughout their life-cycle challenges. Secondly, healthy families proactively nurture their unity and harmony. Thirdly, healthy families find creative ways to talk about their common history and transmit their core values to the next generations.

### The Business Circle

The bottom line in a business is to stay competitive in the marketplace in order to make a profit. The sphere of business activities includes managing and motivating employees, and developing and managing strategy and systems. These business activities require the right mix of effective communication skills, tough decision-making ability, entrepreneurial drive, and attention to detail. One of the most difficult challenges in many businesses is the general human resources task of performance management. This difficulty can be even more pronounced in family firms. It is a rare family business that performs legitimate performance reviews of family members employed in the business.

This failure is a travesty, for it violates the bottom lines of both the family and the business. Members of the younger generation need honest and consistent feedback about their work performance in order to develop new skills and build competence. Regular feedback also affirms their present capacity and skill level. When legitimate performance reviews are not provided, the message being sent is one or all of the following: (a) you are not worth evaluating; (b) we are afraid of what we will find (this is in effect a message of non-confidence); or (c) you are not worth developing as a key employee.

Each of these not so subliminal messages violates the bottom line of the family, namely, to enlarge the circle of love, caring and appreciation. Each of these messages also violates the bottom line of your business, namely, to remain highly competitive. You are not managing well if you are not providing consistent and honest feedback to your employees in order to help them grow in their skill and productivity levels. It's simply bad business practice, and unfortunately it is all too common in family business environments.

### The Ownership Circle

The third intersecting circle—the ownership circle—is often the least understood and talked about within family businesses. Family firms are often referred to as owner-operated businesses. All family members have a sense of that ownership and in all likelihood work as if they had ownership. However, children in family businesses, although they work hard in an ownership-type capacity, often do not have actual shares in the family business and thus have no actual control. Control and power come from ownership. Ownership in family firms often follows the Golden Rule—namely, whoever has the gold makes the rules. The purpose of ownership is the stewardship of equity and values. Owners act responsibly by developing other owners or shareholders, by setting ownership policies and procedures, and by selecting and working with a board of directors or advisors, but the bottom line of ownership remains power and control. What makes this circle especially challenging for many business families is the lack of communication and transparency around the exercise of that power and control.

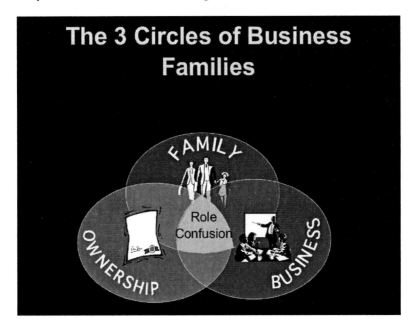

### Role Confusion

The legitimate and essential exercise of power, the skilful management of people and resources, and the gracious and compassionate mutual caring for family members are the three significant roles that can collide to create serious confusion. This role confusion and the subsequent conflict felt internally and within the family business system can account for over 50% of all family business problems. How can we minimize the role confusion and conflict?

First of all, we must honour the different purposes and responsibilities of each circle. The bottom lines of love, money and power have to be understood and appreciated. Secondly, family members need to honour each other's unique aspirations and goals in each of the circles. Some members of the family will choose not to be involved in the business. They need to be given their due respect and also need to be cared for and compassionately supported within the sphere of the family. Too often family businesses relegate family members who have chosen not to be active in the company to second-class status. Thirdly, it is very important for the business family to clarify the core values that bind its members together within all three circles.

Role confusion exists in the intersection of the three separate yet interlocking functions represented by the three circles. Ownership requires serious planning, management requires excellent communication, and family calls for the nurturing of close relationships. Perhaps even more difficult to sort out are the hidden assumptions or "hot buttons" of business partners. Difficult interpersonal dynamics occur whenever an incident, a decision or a conversation seems to be about one thing but is really about something else, namely, love and affirmation, money, or power.

### How Many Hats Can You Wear?

I received a very emotional phone call from a distraught father recounting how he had taken his son-in-law to the woodshed because of a work performance issue. His distress derived from the family's overwhelmingly negative response to what he had done. He felt torn. As he put it, "Am I here to run a business or to run a zoo?" I met with the entire family on a Saturday morning to process what had become a very intractable and volatile family situation. Father, mother, daughter, son-in-law with new baby, and several sons entered the boardroom with coffee percolating and the smell of doughnuts still fresh. Father leaned over to his daughter and said, "Can you get me a cup of coffee?" She exploded. "Get your own —— coffee!" Father looked at me with hands open and said, "What's the problem? All I want is a cup of coffee." What was happening here?

After four hours of discussion, we determined the real issue. The daughter initially explained her outburst by saying, "If Dad really loved me he would've asked my brother to get him the coffee." On the surface this response seemed ridiculous. However, when we probed more deeply we discovered that her anger was tied to her anxiety about returning to the family business after her maternity leave. As a new mother, she felt that her father had given her very little affirmation and she was upset that he had not even discussed her upcoming re-entry into the business with her. The performance-related reprimand that her father had given to her husband reinforced her sense that her father didn't support her. This perception increased her anxiety. Eventually she was able to acknowledge her feelings of insecurity and Dad was able to confess his insensibility to the fear that his lack of communication and support had triggered in his daughter (a key employee).

Dad was experiencing that familiar role confusion between acting as an efficient manager and providing a father's love and support to his daughter. Additionally, his approach to managing a key employee who also happened to be his son-in-law spilled over into the family circle, affecting his relationship with his daughter. The daughter needed love and affirmation; the son-in-law needed firm direction regarding his performance. Dad, like most family business owners, found it difficult to be both father and boss and to do both jobs equally well.

### Money for Love: The High Price of Bad Management

What happens in one circle often affects the dynamics in another circle. Arnie and Ted worked for their father, who was notorious for underpaying both his staff and his sons. Arnie, who was in line to become president, responded to this treatment by behaving in ways that the staff at times found difficult to accept. He could be quite demanding and autocratic, unlike his father, who was rather mild-mannered. As in many workplaces facing leadership changes, resistance took creative forms. The staff undermined Arnie by reporting what they viewed as his unacceptable actions to his father. The issues seemed minor—perceived abuses such as late arrivals and long lunches—but Arnie's father saw them as ample justification for withholding further salary increases from his son. When I talked to Arnie I received a different perspective. Not only was he doing his own job, but he was also handling other office work above and beyond his regular duties. Furthermore, as I talked to his wife I discovered that she too harboured deep bitterness. She had just had a child, the first grandchild in this family, and she was returning to work after a maternity leave. Although she did not object to returning, the tight time frame—just three months after the birth of her baby—made her unhappy. However, financial pressures at home made this early return necessary. She blamed her father-in-law for these pressures because she felt that he was underpaying her husband.

The work-related tensions had ripple effects. Arnie's mother seldom saw her first grandchild during the baby's first year. The tremendous hurt within the family was palpable at every family gathering. This is a classic example of how a poorly handled management issue can spill over into family relationships. It also serves as a fairly typical example of how family members who deeply love one another can run the risk of destroying what they hold most sacred—their family—because of miscommunication and inattention to professional business management.

### Fair vs. Equal

I am sometimes shocked to find farmers without wills. Often these individuals are excellent operators who manage flawless and efficient operations. However, an untimely death without a will could jeopardize the financial viability of their farms and could leave their families in an absolute mess. A common mistake is to attempt to accomplish estate planning through a farm succession strategy. A typical example could involve parents who leave the farm equally to their three children. The situation might be complicated by the fact that only one son actually works on the farm, while the other two children have different professions.

In their attempt to treat all three children equally, the parents could end up sowing the seeds of future family disharmony and farm business failure. Equal does not necessarily mean fair. The next-generation member who has faithfully worked on the farm

> **"It is not wise to use a will as the primary succession planning tool for the family business. A business requires its own succession plan based on the strategic needs of a profitable operation."**

does not regard an equal division of the estate as fair because it disregards his sweat equity. Should all three siblings end up owning the farm operation together, the inactive shareholders could have very different strategic interests than the brother who actually runs the farm. This inevitably leads to conflict down the road.

Three recommendations can help resolve situations of this kind. The first is simply to encourage families to be transparent about the contents of their wills and the intentions of the parents in settling the estate. Secondly, it is not wise to use a will as the primary succession planning tool for the family business. A business requires its own succession plan based on the strategic needs of a profitable operation. Thirdly, those members of the family who wish to own and operate the family business should be allowed to purchase it from the retiring generation. The terms of that business transaction should be duly noted in the original owner's will and should be transparent to the entire family upon any settlement of the estate.

Creativity is desirable when devising plans to divide an estate among the children. One farmer I worked with gave his son, who wished to farm, an early two-million-dollar inheritance in the farm operation. (Interestingly, on average in Canada, two million dollars of equity are required to generate one farm salary.) The father then gave his daughter a roughly equivalent value through a combination of rental property together with a one-million-dollar life insurance policy.

What is significant about this example is that it took the family members almost six months of very intense, open and honest discussions to arrive at this solution and to determine what was really important. They separated the business deal from the inheritance question. It was not a strictly equal deal, but all members of the family felt it was ultimately fair. This family will enjoy getting together at Christmas for a long, long time.

### So, Dad, Who Gets to Be the Boss Now?

A farmer had two sons. Mike was big, strong, decisive and domineering. He was a very good manager and was able to hold himself and other workers accountable for their performance. However, he was quite oppositional and difficult for Dad to deal with. Stan was very intelligent, a good salesman and a smooth and strategic operator. He was not a particularly effective manager of people or of details, but he and his father got along very well. When Dad went on business trips, he especially liked taking Stan along.

Who would succeed Dad in taking over and running a very large and complex agribusiness? Dad was torn. How could he choose one son over the other? The business really needed them both. Dad also had doubts as to whether either of his sons could work for the other.

But perhaps he was asking the wrong question. Many owners are afraid to ask who will succeed them as president. The more important question to ask is the following: What are the strategic needs of the business? How do the gifts of the next generation fit into those strategic needs? If succeeding Dad is of paramount concern, then the family business runs the danger of attempting to clone Dad. Often, however, the family operation has different strategic needs than those present when Dad started the business. The current needs of the business might optimally call for a very different type of management.

The second major problem that can occur when a founder arbitrarily chooses a successor is that the new leader may not receive the kind of support that he or she requires to be successful.

### *There's Nothing Wrong with a Formal Selection Process*

Best-practice recommendations for transitioning operational leadership and selecting the best management for a family business would look like this: Engage the next-generation members of the family in rigorous annual performance reviews for a two-to-four-year period. These reviews may have to be conducted by an outside party in order to be perceived as neutral and fair. Secondly, the family business needs to engage in strategic planning together with key non-family senior managers. Thirdly, the decision-making burden can be formally conducted by an advisory group in order to help the owners, usually the parents, make a final decision which is then not perceived to be an arbitrary call.

In my experience, formalizing the selection process for next-generation leadership positions tends to produce a choice that is best both for the long-term interests of the family business and for long-lasting family harmony. I have seen such a process generate decisions that were different from what the founders had originally envisioned. In the case of the farmer and his two sons, the process also facilitated discussions between those two very competent sons. The conclusion was a fabulously successful company and harmonious family relationships that were fashioned for long-term strategic results. Most importantly, the process took the parents out of the Bermuda triangle of role confusion where their interests as parents and owners intersect.

Juggling love, money and power will always preoccupy business families. To do so successfully requires managing the business according to business principles and interacting with family members on the basis of the family vision. Above all, it is important to remember that estate planning is a family legacy question, whereas succession planning is a strategic business issue. The two concerns are separate and distinct endeavours.

# SECTION II

## INTERGENERATIONAL DYNAMICS: LEARNING TO UNDERSTAND EACH OTHER

# CHAPTER 5

## THE VULNERABILITY
## OF THE NEXT GENERATION

One of my favourite questions to ask an audience is whether they believe that they are adults. The results are surprising. Often people are puzzled. A few gingerly raise their hands. Eventually many more people may put up their hands. The uncertainty surrounding this question is an indication of the difficulty Western society in general has with the status and definition of adulthood. What does it mean to be an adult? For those people who think they are adults, what are their perceptions?

Does adulthood mean the right to legally drink? Does adulthood mean that you have graduated from high school? Or does it occur when you get married? Or when you take your first job? Are you an adult when you have children? The most common answer goes something like this: adults are people who are responsible, are able to manage their finances, are independent, and are contributors to their society.

In more traditional societies of four hundred years ago, individuals became adults once they reached puberty, which for most young people was between the ages of eleven and fifteen. They were then married off and became part of society, functioning as emerging adults. Becoming an adult was a carefully prescribed process that involved taking one's place in the dominant culture and functioning in patterned and acceptable ways. However, the modern Western world is ambivalent about the entire period between adolescence and adulthood. It is a time with few benchmarks and signposts to guide young people in their journey towards adulthood.

My working definition of an adult is "someone who has the ability to make genuine choices." That ability is easily compromised and can be quite difficult to develop in a family business setting. For next-generation members of business families, the process of

> **"My working definition of an adult is 'someone who has the ability to make genuine choices.'"**

becoming an adult is complicated because making genuine choices can seem harder when the work environment is controlled by the older generation. Although decision-making can be difficult in any family, in situations where professional life and livelihood are controlled by the family there is an extra power differential that makes it more challenging for young people to make meaningful decisions and therefore feel and act like true adults.

A more technical definition of adulthood is "the ability to achieve psychological distance from one's family of origin." Another way to state this idea is to say that becoming an adult means finding one's own voice—not the voice of one's parents or peers, but one's own voice. This definition is closely tied to the concept of "life stage development" (see chart, opposite page). The stages outlined on this chart are perhaps the most significant diagnostic tool for understanding family dynamics and assessing the potential vulnerabilities of individuals within business families.

Historical multidisciplinary research conducted by Erickson, Piaget, Kohlberg, et al. and popularized in books like Gail Sheehy's *Passages*[1] has carefully chronicled our journey through the various stages of life. From the smooth skin of a newborn baby to

# Lifecycle Development • Choices and Challenges

| Challenge | Life Task |
|---|---|
| **AGE 0–12 STAGE CHILDHOOD** | |
| Learn to trust | Autonomy vs. shame |
| Learn to work | Industry vs. inferiority |
| Learn to take initiative | Self-esteem vs. guilt |
| **AGE 13–18 STAGE ADOLESCENCE** | |
| Finding one's own voice | Identity vs. role confusion |
| **AGE 19–26 STAGE THE CRITICAL YEARS** | |
| Establish psychological distance from family | Intimacy vs. isolation |
| **AGE 27–33 STAGE EARLY ADULTHOOD** | |
| Explore occupational and interpersonal roles | Seek success and mastery vs. failure |
| **AGE 34–39 STAGE CHOOSING ONE'S OWN PATH** | |
| Deepen commitments to occupational and social roles | Attain recognition, advancement and security |
| Establish family and home | Competency vs. stagnation |
| **AGE 40–45 STAGE MID-LIFE** | |
| Aware of physical mortality | Come to terms with limitations |
| Reconsider future | vs. despair or escape |
| **AGE 46–55 STAGE MIDDLE ADULTHOOD** | |
| Creating the legacy | Sustain mental and physical |
| Calmer time | health while facing aging process |
| **AGE 56+ STAGE LATE ADULTHOOD** | |
| Deal with retirement | Come to terms with life |
| Seek meaningful activities | Pass on authority |
| Find integrity | Plan the second half of your life |

the wrinkles of our wise elders, our human development has been charted from cradle to grave. We know what will happen at each step of life's journey at three distinct levels: psychological and emotional, physical, and cognitive. It is the interplay of all three that determines how we handle the challenges and life tasks outlined on the chart. Successfully navigating these challenges and life tasks during the appropriate chronological sequence provides the foundation for navigating the challenges of the next stage of life well. Failure to address the challenges inherent in a given life stage often results in difficulty managing the corresponding life tasks of that particular stage. For example, a toddler who suffers abuse grows up never learning to trust. With that developmental building block damaged, this child will almost certainly move into subsequent life stages with a sense of shame rather than autonomy; feeling inferior; and coping with major self-esteem issues. These issues will have a major impact on his or her ability to establish healthy, trusting relationships as an adult and will most probably hamper work and career performance. We use the shorthand term "being stuck" to describe such an individual.

The three most difficult stages of life for individuals in family firms are the *critical years* (journey into adulthood); *mid-life* (reaffirmation of adult identity and responsibilities); and *retirement* (search for meaning and integrity while moving into the longest phase of life). The chronological age ranges associated with these stages are fluid, but generally the critical years are from eighteen to thirty, mid-life covers the period from thirty-five to forty-five, and retirement is the stage from age fifty-five to seventy.

Finding one's voice as an adult in a family business can be quite difficult within the context of successful succession planning. It takes healthy adults sitting across the table from one another to negotiate a plan that (1) makes sense and (2) will actually stick. Success requires that they sit and talk to one another. It can also mean that one family member uses his or her voice on behalf of other family members who might not have functioning voices. Individuals gain personal power through their voices: the power to be heard, to be understood, to make a difference, to move into friendships and to negotiate for what they truly believe is right and fair.

I have heard many next-generation sons and daughters pour out their hearts and bemoan family members who do not listen to them. Some describe families that ignore their ideas for improving the business or dismiss them out of hand. Their suggestions for workflow improvements are ignored. Or they might feel dominated by a very vocal mother or a competitive brother.

### The Son Who Lost His Voice

While observing a son within his family business setting, I noticed some patterns that I see very regularly. The first was that the entire family never talked openly about disagreements; everyone seemed afraid of conflict. The message this son had taken from his family of origin was that it was not okay to disagree. If you did have a differing opinion you were somehow violating family etiquette. Secondly, as with many other young people who have not found their voices, this son just didn't communicate very much. It was as if his larynx had constricted and he had lost his ability to speak. Perhaps he had never found it in the first place. When he did timidly venture an opinion during a facilitated meeting, he sounded completely bottled up and hoarse. Thirdly, and what is interesting in many of these situations, the parents complained that their son seemed quite angry—and in fact he was angry much of the time. They often talked about a blue cloud that seemed to follow him around wherever he went.

When you have difficulty expressing what you truly desire, when you have difficulty expressing your honest feelings, you run the risk of becoming trapped. People who feel trapped find some way to escape. If next-generation children cannot give voice to their feelings, thoughts and desires, they find expression in other ways. Common substitutes are the abuse of alcohol, uncontrollable anger and rage, drug use, gambling and overeating. Addictive patterns of behaviour among children of family businesses are occurring in epidemic proportions. Anecdotal evidence coming from the U.S. indicates that children of family businesses are ten times more likely than the normal population to move into addictive patterns of behaviour. The reason for these destructive patterns is developmental. During the critical years—usually between the ages of eighteen and thirty, when young people are attempting to become adults and are establishing some psychological distance from their families—the family business draws them into its orbit. The invitation to become involved is usually extended with the best intentions. But often in allowing their children to enter the family business before they have achieved a measure of adulthood, namely, the ability to make choices that are genuinely their own, the parents unwittingly trap their children.

For these children, the entire discussion about succession then becomes another daunting challenge in which the power differential is sometimes overwhelming. These succession discussions can become simply another occasion for the next-generation members to feel that they have no power, or to display once again their lack of confidence. This disempowering scenario can often prompt the next-generation members to feel ashamed of their cowardice, of not being able to speak up for themselves. The difficulty in making a genuine choice is evident in their lack of a voice, and this triggers an attempt to find ways of achieving success in the areas of their life that are not controlled by their parents. They often do so in school courses, through outside work experiences, or through volunteer activities. Best-practice recommendations for family businesses indicate that next-generation members should acquire a large chunk of experience away from the family firm before making a decision, a genuine decision, to join the family operation permanently. In fact, it is recommended that members of the next generation gain at least three to five years of outside work experience before attempting to join the family business. Otherwise they are in danger of making a decision that is not genuine.

Finding one's voice is difficult at the best of times. But in a business family an independent sense of self-confidence can be even harder to achieve. At the end of the day it is this sense of self-con-

> **"It is recommended that members of the next generation gain at least three to five years of outside work experience before attempting to join the family business."**

fidence that makes someone a successful leader of the family business, if that is what he or she aspires to. It is this sense of self-confidence that will allow him or her to feel like an adult on an equal footing with other members of the family.

Three questions need to be asked and answered successfully before we can feel like an adult. Am I lovable? Am I competent? Am I in control of my own life? Our earliest sense of being loved and competent comes from our parents and usually from our family of origin. In fact, the ability to take initiative and the ability to trust are life tasks that for most humans are accomplished by approximately age five, according to developmental researchers. They are

> **"Three questions need to be asked and answered successfully before we can feel like an adult. Am I lovable? Am I competent? Am I in control of my own life?"**

the building blocks of normal human growth. When a little child cries, is hungry or has a wet diaper and her mother takes care of her, she feels loved and enveloped by a complete circle of care and trust. Our earliest sense of competence usually comes from managing chores successfully at home, being able to master basic life skills such as putting our clothes on, keeping ourselves clean, managing to arrive for appointments on time, and being obedient to our parents. From about age two, however, an innate drive for independence begins to assert itself. The Terrible Twos and the rebellious teen years are but the precursors of a later time in life in which we take fuller control of our destiny. That taking control usually means some type of separation from our parents and our family of origin.

Growing up in a business family inevitably means that a positive response to all three questions—"Am I lovable? Am I com-

> *"Within business families the unwritten and sometimes unspoken promise that 'someday this will all be yours' functions as golden handcuffs, trapping the next generation in jobs and roles within the family business."*

petent? Am I in control of my own life?—depends on one's family of origin. Many parents do not realize how much power and control they consciously and unconsciously wield over their children, particularly during the critical years from eighteen to twenty-six. Within business families the unwritten and sometimes unspoken promise that "someday this will all be yours" functions as golden handcuffs, trapping the next generation in jobs and roles within the family business.

I see too many young people who, having attained very good income streams, having risen to significant management roles far exceeding their level of education or experience, having started a young family, having amassed a fair amount of debt, wake up one morning realizing that they do not enjoy what they are doing, probably could not get the same amount of money working else-where, and resent the fact that they are collecting their "allowance" or salary from their parents. Many of them feel totally trapped.

### Trapped With Golden Handcuffs?

What happens when you feel trapped? You usually attempt to escape. The most common escapes involve alcohol and drugs. Depression and out-of-control rage are also very common. As mentioned earlier, addictive patterns such as driving too fast, sexual addictions, gambling, eating disorders and Internet romances are all symptoms of feeling trapped and helpless with no voice to articulate one's feelings and assert control over and against the parents and family who are supposed to love and take care of you. However, by the age of thirty or forty, individuals shouldn't feel the need to be taken care of any longer. They need to get on with their own lives, establish their own intimate connections, and feel competent because of what they have accomplished and not because they happen to be the owner's son or daughter. As one of my clients screamed, pounding the table in tears as he rued the day he joined the family business, "I'm tired of being called Hank's boy."

One of the most significant adult choices is the selection of a life partner. Yet in my work with business families I often receive some version of the following request from parents: "Can you please come and fix our daughter-in-law? If only our son had not married this woman. She makes him so surly. Now that he's married he has become so uncooperative. He was never that way before. Why is it that our daughter-in-law is keeping our son away from us? We don't deserve this kind of rejection." I do not want to minimize the legitimate sources of conflict and the deep-seated differences or even personality clashes that can exist in every family. But it is often too easy to pick on the in-laws or "outlaws," as they are often affectionately called.

The real difficulty for these parents is often that of coping with change. They find it difficult to accept that their son or daughter has chosen a life partner and that their child's loyalty is now shifting towards his or her own nuclear family. This evolution is entirely normal and needs to happen. However, the new loyalty could at times conflict with the unquestioning loyalty desired by parents. The real difficulty for members of the next generation is that they also want a measure of control over their own futures. Now that they have separate lives and children, they are beginning to think and dream about what their children will someday become and how they will provide for their family. In the meantime, they don't relish the reality of having to negotiate with their parents whenever they need a pay raise, which to them can feel like a handout.

If a common request by parents is to "please fix" our daughter-in-law or son-in-law, then one of the most common requests from the next generation is for someone to tell them where they are going, especially when there is no succession planning in place. Unfortunately, many parents interpret this question as an attack and feel that their children are ungrateful and moving way too quickly. In reality the next-generation members are attempting in a very healthy way to assert some control over their own futures and their own lives. We all have to remember that in a family business we cannot fix each other, but we can all learn to be more tolerant of changes and more accepting of each others' vulnerabilities during natural life-stage transitions. This critical life-stage transition towards becoming an adult is probably the most difficult one for business families to navigate.

### Conclusion

Managing life tasks during our various stages of development is a cumulative process. Failure to navigate certain tasks well has the effect of depleting the reservoir of relational capital available to both individuals and their respective families. There is a technical term—"individuation"—used to define healthy development into adulthood. Lack of proper individuation as outlined in this chapter results in family members who have difficulty establishing their own identity and sense of self-worth independent of their family. Their personal dreams and goals tend to become enmeshed with the dreams and goals of their family. During the "critical years," the family business can function in ways that either promote or retard the children's healthy choices. Poor individuation often leads to stagnation in work performance and can eventually result in serious depression. Destructive addictive behaviour is not uncommon among next-generation children who have had difficulty coming to terms with normal life tasks because they feel trapped.

The potential for conflict among family members and between generations is also likely to surface in more destructive ways during three distinct stages. These developmental stages coincide with three periods in the family business cycle. The first stage occurs during the successor's entry into the family business. The second occurs during the succession planning process. The third occurs during the retirement of the founder.

Significant research on father and son relationships in family businesses shows that there are predictable periods in which the individual cycles either mesh well or create conflict:[2]

| Implications of Life Stage Theory for Succession Success | | |
| --- | --- | --- |
| Age of Founder | Age of Next Generation | Prognosis |
| 40–50 | Early 20s | Problematic |
| 51–60 | 26–33 | Harmonious |
| 60s | 35–45 | Problematic |

### Problematic Period (40–50 / Early 20s)

Next-generation members in their early twenties are energetic and ambitious, yet naïve and inexperienced. Children are usually willing and eager to take risks, whereas parents could be in a period of consolidation. Conflict over how to run the business is often inevitable. Interactions within the business serve as an unconscious forum for family members to test their more intrinsic sense of feeling loved, appreciated and respected, and of feeling competent and in control of their own lives.

### Harmonious Period (51–60 / 26–33)

Next-generation members are more mature and often preoccupied with establishing their own nuclear families. Founders have hopefully dealt with their mid-life transitional issues and are more settled and able to function as mentors and coaches to their children as they transition into the business. There is usually a greater potential for mutually supportive relationships during this stage, and succession planning isn't as loaded with the need to control, feel respected and gain more appreciation.

### Problematic Period (60s / 35–45)

If the next generation has not acquired control of the business or the family business has not achieved certainty regarding a defined succession plan by the time the younger members are in mid-life, frustration can be quite pronounced. Meanwhile, the founding members are facing the difficult transition of retirement and all the loss-of-control and identity subtexts that surface for them emotionally. This can be a volatile time for business families.

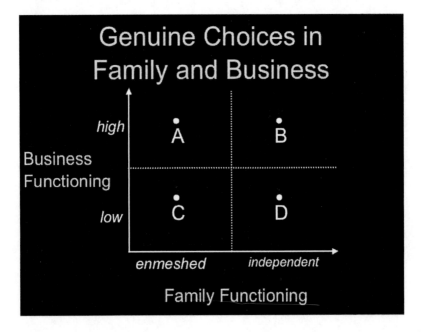

### Genuine Choices in Family and Business

As shown in the chart on the preceding page, the ways in which families and businesses function affect each other in predictable ways:

A. Firms in this quadrant tend to be quite contentious. Often run by an imperious president, these families will also have significant sibling rivalry. Family firms in quadrant A may seek out and require extra legal services.

B. Family firms that rank high in terms of both business functioning and healthy growth towards independence of their members tend to engage in healthy conflict. They also manage transitions successfully by having succession plans, strategic business plans and estate plans in place.

C. This quadrant is filled with more dysfunctional business families. It contains families dealing with business performance issues as well as individual family members who cannot seem to achieve independent adulthood. Experienced family business consultants report a high incidence of substance abuse among these clients. One of the pioneers in family business consulting, David Bork, used an alcoholic family as the case example for his book *Family Business, Risky Business* (1986).[3]

D. Family firms in this quadrant tend to be more passive, with a greater number of individual members leaving the family business to pursue their own dreams and professions. Many of these family firms end up being sold to non–family members. These companies may have more business-related issues than interpersonal ones.

# CHAPTER 6

## COMMUNICATING WITH EMOTIONAL INTELLIGENCE

A study of three hundred leading American executives conducted by the Harvard Business School a number of years ago tried to ascertain what had made them successful.[1] The study examined three criteria for success. One was the influence of cognitive intelligence, or IQ. The second was the contribution of various skill sets, and the third was the role of EQ, or emotional intelligence. The authors were amazed at the results, which showed that over 80% of the success of these high-functioning executives could be attributed to their emotional intelligence. The influence of high IQs and accumulated skill sets paled in comparison.

The study of emotional intelligence has become something of a cottage industry during the last decade. The three leading researchers in this area are Mayer and Salovey,[2] Bar-On[3] and Goleman.[4] Their investigations of EQ seek to understand how individuals perceive, understand, utilize and manage their emotions in an effort to predict and foster personal effectiveness. The most recent research by Goleman in 2002 shows that the more senior the leader, the more important emotional competency becomes.

Successful business families are usually emotionally intelligent. They have a high EQ. Many individuals within high-functioning families have the ability to convert their feelings into manageable facts by engaging in the necessary but sometimes difficult conversations that uncover the free-floating assumptions within any family system. Yet too many family firms have buried feelings that operate as secrets in a way that prevents them from addressing questions of succession or business roles openly. A major step in beginning either the succession journey or strategic planning is for family members to understand and manage their individual and collective feelings, to honestly express their true desires and needs, and sometimes to openly and safely disagree with one another. Business families that are able to accomplish these tasks can be considered emotionally intelligent, and their members also tend to be lifelong learners.

What does it mean to be emotionally intelligent? According to Goleman in *Primal Leadership*, there are four quadrants that establish emotional intelligence: self-awareness, self-management, social awareness, and relationship management (see chart).

# Emotional Intelligence

| Self Awareness | Social Awareness |
|---|---|
| Self Management | Relationship Management |

### EQ and Self-Awareness

Foundational to emotional self-awareness is the ability to be attuned to one's inner signals. Are you able to communicate openly about your emotions? The ability to read oneself emotionally depends upon accurate self-assessment. Our earliest and most consistent sources of information about ourselves tend to come from our immediate family. Our parents and siblings give us clues about ourselves in their interactions with us, and we begin to define ourselves according to the affection, criticism, praise and overall feedback they give to us in a variety of situations. As we grow older and more mature we get more accurate assessments of ourselves through our report cards at school, our performance reviews at work, and the feedback we receive from other relationships.

In this way we begin to identify our limitations and our strengths. Some of us do more work on self-assessment by engaging in personality profiling exercises or by arranging executive coaching. These tools and exercises all enhance the ability to see oneself accurately and help to more quickly identify both the areas in our life needing growth and the giftedness which we possess. People with high EQ develop a sense of humour about themselves and their strengths and weaknesses. They also develop high self-confidence and welcome the difficult assignments that can play to their strengths.

Emotionally intelligent business families are characterized by the attention they give to understanding themselves as individuals and as a family system in two particular ways. Each of the family members must have a fairly accurate assessment of his or her dominant personality trait or style and how this affects his or her communication patterns. Business families that are able to understand, tolerate and "style flex" with each other's personality styles and quirks are business families that can express and communicate more honestly and freely around all kinds of business and family issues. It all starts with accurate self-knowledge.

The second characteristic is that highly emotionally intelligent families can regard each other and work with each other without judging differences in style and personality. Quick and pervasive judgement destroys partnerships. Emotionally intelligent business families develop a collective self-confidence that comes from being able to successfully navigate conflict and steer through difficult moments in their family and business life.

### Managing Emotional Anxiety

Anxiety stems from difficulties in managing our fears. The inability to identify and name deep-seated feelings of inadequacy, anger, betrayal and low self-worth can bring on dysfunctional feelings of shame later in life. During one family gathering I observed the daughter of the business owner cowering close to the coffee maker and occupying herself with pouring coffee during times of intense conflict among family members. By taking on this routine role she seemed to absolve herself of the responsibility to participate in the intense discussions around the table. She was clearly frightened and very anxious. Although in her forties with a family of her own, she still seemed to have no voice in her family of origin. It didn't surprise me when I received a phone call from her soon afterwards informing me that she had left her husband after twenty years of marriage and asking for advice on what she should do next. Her symptoms, which included irritable bowel syndrome and skin rashes coupled with alcohol problems and depression, were all indications that she was not able to identify and speak about the emotional turmoil within her. The effect of her low EQ was manifesting itself in both marital and parenting relationships.

To her credit, she began to work at understanding herself better and identifying the triggers for her anxiety and emotional and communication withdrawal patterns, particularly during times of intense conflict. The long-term danger in ignoring our emotions is that we tend to find other patterns of behaviour to fill the void. These other patterns tend to be destructive addictive patterns.

### Uncontrollable Emotions

Male anxiety patterns tend to be more aggressive. One family business owner, president of a very successful international firm, was attempting to implement a succession plan with his three children, all of whom had significant and responsible roles within the family business. Having concluded (accurately) that he lacked the ability to cope effectively with his impending retirement and the transfer of control in the business he had founded, this owner engaged the services of numerous professionals to facilitate the succession process for his family. Although he did not confess his deep anxiety about the looming changes in both his business and his personal life, his behaviour and communication patterns, particularly within his own family, often became quite controlling. The larger picture remained a very successful one, and a succession plan was both developed and implemented, but there were moments along the way when out-of-control emotions nearly derailed the process. Instructive in this case is the fact that the family members' EQ levels gyrated between extreme highs and low lows. The anxiety patterns within this family also manifested themselves in significant addictive behaviours.

### EQ and Self-Management

Once we have acquired a better knowledge of ourselves, we need to learn how to manage ourselves better. Almost all of us struggle with some level of anger and impulse control at times. Individuals with higher EQ have learned to manage their anger in productive ways and to work at impulse control in healthy ways as well. They are therefore able to stay calm and clear-headed under stress.

Self-management requires us to practise a level of transparency and authentic openness toward others about our feelings, our beliefs and our actions. People with high EQ can admit their mistakes and their faults.

Self-management also requires adaptability. The ability to juggle multiple demands without losing focus or energy is a skill set that can be developed. The emotional ability and willingness to be flexible is a deeper strength for building EQ.

High-EQ performers are achievement-driven and constantly seek performance improvements. They also look for ways to learn and to teach others about what they have learned in order to accomplish more and achieve excellence.

Another clear strength of high-EQ performers is the ability to take initiative and to seize or create opportunities. Optimism about the future is a hallmark of persons who manage themselves well. They welcome change and expect changes to be positive for them.

It is an axiom in business that we cannot manage others until we have learned to manage ourselves. When one looks at compatibility among family business partners, the traits of self-control, transparency, adaptability, achievement, initiative and optimism are critical to long-term success.

### EQ and Social Awareness

Social awareness begins with empathy. Just as emotional self-awareness helps us to identify and speak about our own feelings, so empathy tunes us in to the emotional signals of those around us. Empathy is the ability to see a situation from another person's point of view. It is the ability to get along with people of diverse backgrounds, cultures and frames of reality.

Persons with high emotional intelligence also exhibit a fair degree of organizational awareness. Some might call this characteristic "being political." But being politically astute is really the ability to detect important social networks and power relationships.

Recognition of the importance of customer service and the prioritizing of customer satisfaction have always been hallmarks of high-EQ management.

### Relationship Management

Inspiring one's coworkers and staff with a compelling vision and a shared mission is probably the first and foremost challenge of any business leader. Employees usually rally around a common purpose that is larger than day-to-day survival and individual greed.

High-EQ leaders exert influence rather than control. They are able to achieve and build buy-in to the organization's mission and goals and they are usually very persuasive within teams and groups.

Successful leaders usually develop other successful leaders. They do this by understanding other people's goals, strengths and weaknesses. They are not afraid to give timely and constructive feedback.

High-EQ managers often function as catalysts for change. They are able to recognize the need for change and actually enjoy challenging the status quo.

Because of their effectiveness in defining a common goal and vision for the company, high-EQ leaders are also good at redirecting divergent energy towards that common goal. They are able to draw in different parties and different perspectives and thereby manage conflict very effectively.

An emphasis on teamwork and collaboration sets high-EQ leaders apart. When the family business workplace is well-run, it tends to have a friendly atmosphere and a collegial tone. The management style is one of building and strengthening close relationships rather than simply enforcing work obligations.

### Summary of EQ

Despite volumes of research indicating that EQ is correlated with personality traits having a genetic component, recent studies have suggested that EQ can be improved with sustained effort and a systematic program. At the Weatherhead School of Management at Case Western Reserve University, the MBA program specifically addresses EQ issues and includes a required course on competence building. Research is showing that EQ competencies can be significantly improved and that the improvements are sustainable over time. These findings are noteworthy because traditional MBA programs achieve little or no sustained EQ improvement.[5]

Business families with emotional intelligence are cognizant of the changing voices within the family. Healthy families also work very hard at helping the younger members develop their voices. Within families there can be three types of voices: a child's voice, a parent's voice and adult voices. We have all heard the high-pitched voices of children insisting "No, I don't want to" or "It's not fair" or "It's his fault" or "I didn't do it." The words often reflect blame shifting, a sense of victimization, oppositional attitudes and, of course, an unwillingness to take responsibility for one's own actions. We expect these words, gestures and thoughts from little children. However, it is disconcerting and dangerous when similar "children's" voices are still heard within the family business context from children in their thirties and forties.

The parental voice has two dominant tones. One is comforting and supportive; the other is more controlling. "Make your bed" or "Clean your room" or "Why did you miss your curfew?" or "Get dressed" are among the commands expressed by parental voices in many homes. But we also hear "Let me fix that ouchie" or "Let me help you with that homework." The parental voice, whether meant to comfort or control, remains a voice of domination and power, essentially relegating the person being addressed to a subservient role. In most cases this voice loses much of its effectiveness once children reach their teens.

The only voice that is effective over time is an adult voice. Calm and rational, the adult voice uses logic to ask questions and frames comments with lots of "I statements." It acknowledges and respects the adult voice and the intention to take responsibility in other members of the family. It does not begin with judgement and the need to control, but seeks dialogue and problem-solving solutions that will enhance the dignity and interdependence of each family member.

Emotionally intelligent families predominantly employ their adult voices when communicating with one another. Their communication is characterized by dialogue rather than control.

### Intergenerational Differences: Trigger Points
One of the difficulties in completing a successful family business transition is that the new generation often has a different point of

view on how to run the business. The founders obviously know how to start a business, but they may not have learned how to manage a business after it has grown to a certain size. This situation can lead to serious intergenerational conflict over the future strategic direction of the operation. Senior family members often talk about dedication and hard work, by implication criticizing the next generation for unwillingness to put in the long hours that they did. Members of the next generation tend to argue for more work-family balance. Their differentiating arguments talk about professionalizing the operation. In other words, they also implicitly judge their parents—because what the parents hear is that the next generation is going to work "smarter rather than harder."

### Next-Generation Accountability and Professionalism

Two brothers had managed to amass thousands of acres of farmland and one of the largest dairy herds in their province through sheer hard work, determination and some timely buying of quotas. They regularly worked eighty to one hundred hours a week. Their long-term plan was to transition their agribusiness to a consortium of five cousins. The two brothers believed that if the five next-generation family members also worked eighty to one hundred hours a week, the farming operation would be just as successful as when they were in charge.

There were two large problems with their assumptions. Firstly, what if the next-generation members want to be even more successful than the founding members? Accepting this possibility is actually a little more difficult than it sounds. Family business research shows that one of the major reasons fathers find it so difficult to relinquish control is the subconscious fear that the next generation may learn to operate their business more successfully than they have.

The second problem is one of work-family balance. Members of the younger generation often do not share the workaholic attitudes of their parents. Not that they don't work hard—but their experience as children of founders causes them to desire a different quality of home life than they experienced growing up. The presenting problem during intergenerational transfers is that this different point of view is perceived as personal criticism by their parents. The next generation rightly perceives that in order to accomplish their objectives for the business, they will have to manage assets and growth and cash flow in a much more professional manner than their parents might have done. The younger generation often calls this process "professionalism" or "professionalizing the business." The senior generation just sees it as more overhead expenses.

The two farming brothers were eventually able to transfer their agribusiness to the consortium of cousins. Without a doubt, the success of this transfer was due to the implementation of new management practices. Rather than dwelling on the question of who was working harder, the two generations were able to focus on operational efficiency and introduced a number of best practices, including formal biweekly management meetings, the development of a strategic plan with actual job descriptions, and an annual budgeting process with projections. They developed an accountability structure that formalized a way of measuring performance.

This approach depersonalized the process and removed much of the emotion when performance reviews and evaluations of family members took place. Also crucial to their success during the first year of transition was the introduction of new, professional patterns in their communication procedures and in their management structure. The involvement of third-party facilitators during this time was key to keeping conversations on track and productive. Once the operational accountability structures were in place and the cousins had demonstrated that they could run the agribusiness profitably, the senior brothers had no difficulty in transferring the ownership shares because of their newfound confidence.

### *"Not Enough Group Hugs"*

After one of my visits to a family business client, the oldest son returned to the shop. A key employee asked him, "Who was that stranger and what was going on?" The son replied, "He's a consultant that the family has hired." "So what is this consultant telling you?" inquired the employee. (The son emphasized that this employee happened to be very prickly and somewhat paranoid.) "Well," drawled the son, "he says that we just don't have enough group hugs around here!" With a twinkle in his eye and much laughter he shared his difficulty in convincing this employee not to resign.

Ironically, the son had hit on a key vulnerability of family businesses. Lack of appreciation has long been recognized as a serious

> ## "Lack of appreciation is the leading cause of family business disharmony."

issue that can destroy family business harmony. There just doesn't seem to be enough appreciation to go around.

In preliminary discussions around family kitchen tables, I eventually ask family members a very basic question: "How are you being acknowledged or appreciated for your efforts so that you can feel valued?" Too often I receive back only blank stares. In one situation a mother finally answered with some trepidation: "We just don't do that around here." Appreciation? Acknowledgement? Feeling valued? Another husband, who wondered aloud at the purpose of the question, responded, "My wife knows I love her because I told her that when we got married." This particular couple had been married for over thirty years. Could it be that he had not told her he loved her during that entire time?

There is a generation of business owners and parents who believe that withholding praise builds character. Others simply don't give the matter much thought. Parents often explain to me, "Our kids know they are appreciated—we don't have to tell them." I emphasize to these individuals that this attitude and style of parenting is simply wrong-headed. It is developmentally inappropriate and psychologically damaging, particularly for young people who thrive on appreciation and who need regular, consistent and specific affirmation in order to build self-confidence.

I am not sure whether family businesses need "more group hugs." But I am convinced that family business members need to work much more intentionally and intensively at demonstrating and articulating mutual appreciation for each other. This ability is the foundation for emotionally intelligent communication. And it is the essential key to family harmony and family business success at all levels of engagement.

## Emotional Intelligence and Economic Decision-Making

Self-control is one of the key components of emotional intelligence and it is fundamental to consistent decision-making. Yet it is difficult to maintain, and research suggests that energy spent exercising self-control in one situation reduces later efforts at self-control.

One study by R.F. Baumeister[6] asked three groups of participants to arrive in a state of hunger (no food for three hours prior to the experiment). Members of the first group were directed to a room in which the smell of freshly baked chocolate chip cookies was overpowering. The room contained two trays, one bearing the freshly baked cookies and chocolate treats, the other piled high with radishes. Group members were instructed to eat as many radishes as they could in five minutes, but were told not to touch the cookies. Members of the second group were taken to a similar room with the same two food choices and were told that they could eat the cookies. The third group simply sat in an empty room. After five minutes all food was removed and all participants were given intriguing but unsolvable problems to solve. The objective of the study was to measure the amount of time that elapsed before participants gave up, and the number of attempts they made before that happened.

The results were astounding. The individuals who had been told to eat radishes but not cookies had presumably expended a great deal of self-control in resisting the treats. On average they spent less than half as much time attempting to solve the problems compared to those who had eaten the cookies or nothing at all. They also made far fewer attempts to solve the problems before giving up. Baumeister summarized his research as follows:

1. Emotional distress results in failure to think things through and leads to high-risk behaviour and poor choices.
2. People whose self-esteem is threatened tend to lose their capacity to regulate themselves. Their need to recover wounded pride often overrides their normal rational decision-making.
3. People can regulate themselves only to a limited extent. There seems to be a finite amount of self-regulatory strength or energy available. When it fails or is depleted, people move more quickly to self-defeating behaviour.
4. Interpersonal rejection causes irrational and self-defeating behaviour to become more common. The need to belong is such a key component of our well-being that when it is not met, our ability to self-regulate and resist impulsive decision-making is reduced.

# CHAPTER 7

# "FOUNDERITIS" AND THE CHALLENGE OF HEALTHY AGING

*"At fifteen I set my heart upon learning,*
*At thirty I established myself in accordance with ritual,*
*At forty I no longer had perplexities,*
*At fifty I knew the mandate of heaven,*
*At sixty I was at ease with whatever I heard,*
*At seventy I could follow my heart's desire without*
*transgressing the boundaries of right."* – Confucius

"Founderitis" can be defined as the state of needing to be in control of what you have founded. Unfortunately Murphy's Law indicates that the longer one stays in control, the more likely the chance that the business one has founded will be destroyed.

Many in the so-called "boomer generation" are being bombarded with retirement information. On occasion we are all asked what we will do when we retire. The responses range from abject fear of the question to unbridled fantasy projections. Most of us are somewhere in between. But the entire notion of retirement doesn't make a lot of sense to many persons who have established and built businesses. The word retirement conjures up an image of the first nail being hammered into our coffin. Thus the emotional fear of coping with retirement becomes one of the largest barriers for family businesses when it comes to succession planning.

The difficulty for many is really the fear of change. Most business owners understand, whether consciously or unconsciously, that succession will necessitate a transfer of power and control. That process forces us to examine some very core self-understandings. If, at age fifty-five to sixty-five, an individual's sense of being a lovable person, a competent person and a person in control of his own life depends upon his identity as a business owner, then the horizon called retirement can loom as a very dangerous and fearful place. Business owners who feel positive about these questions—Am I lovable? Am I competent? Am I in control of my own life?—can usually get on with succession and transfer of control and can effect a very smooth transition of their operations. However, if they feel inadequate in any of these three areas, then succession planning can become an attempt to boost their feelings about themselves rather than an exercise in strategic business management.

I prefer not to use the word retirement in describing the transition that owners face from one stage of life to the next. Instead I talk about redirecting our energies and our lifestyle. We need to understand and acknowledge that this is a rather difficult time, particularly for men, who have traditionally had more difficulty coping with change than women.

There are some very real reasons for the difficulty family business owners have in giving up control of the process of change. Here are the top seven:

### #7 – People Die Soon After They Retire
Many founders believe that people die soon after they retire. Statistically this is nonsense. However, almost everybody has an anecdote to support this fear. Based on preliminary research, the only people who tend to die soon after retirement are blue-collar workers who have worked in the same capacity for over thirty-five years. Still, the fear of dying is real for many business owners and keeps them from initiating any kind of succession planning.

### #6 – I Hate Gardening, Golf and Tennis

Many business owners would claim that they hate gardening, golf and tennis. They have not cultivated many hobbies in their relentless pursuit of family business excellence. Many of them would not know what to do with their time if they actually effected a transition and were no longer needed in the office every day.

### #5 – I Need Some Place to Go

Business owners become habituated to their place of work. They need a place to go. They may have married their spouses in sickness and in health and for plenty and in want. However, their partners did not bargain with having lunch and dinner with their spouses every day during retirement. In many successful family business transitions, some type of semi-permanent or permanent office arrangement for the departing founder is necessary to seal the deal. Whether it is the freedom to walk the acreage on the farm that they have so lovingly nurtured and grown or the opportunity to read the financial news in that corner office on the third floor, founders need reassurance that they will have some place to go. For many of them, that physical location is inextricably connected with their own sense of identity and well-being.

### #4 – The Kids Want to Change the Business

Perhaps the kids want to change the way the business is run. The thought of the next generation instituting major changes in their business can send some business owners around the bend. Founders have often nurtured a group of managers and staff to whom they are very loyal. One of their fears is that when the members of the next generation take over, they will not want to retain all of these employees. It is very common for key advisers and staff to be changed during and after family business successions, in part because the next-generation members want to assert their own authority and control. Unfortunately, the response of the founders can be trepidation and resistance.

### #3 – How Do I Choose Among My Children?

For parents who have several capable children, there is often a reluctance to choose one to succeed them as president. There are too many examples of owners making a decision and then watching all hell break loose. The success or failure of this step depends on the timing of the decision and the decision-making process used. One father in his seventies sat in my office with a number of his children and proceeded to inform the family that the fourth-oldest son would succeed him as leader of the company. Everyone in the room was hearing this information for the first time. The oldest son, who thought that he was in line for the post, was clearly outraged. The mother hung her head in shame because she knew that the decision would mean serious rifts in the family. There was more trouble ahead in the form of another sibling, the current financial leader of the company, who was not present at the meeting and who felt that she would be the anointed leader of the company.

The effect was disastrous for both the family and the business. There are two lessons to be learned from examples like this: Do not wait too long to start the leadership succession process within the business. Secondly, consider implementing a formal leadership succession protocol. The most successful transitions include a clearly defined way of choosing a next-generation leader whose qualities, commitments and experience are the right fit for the strategic needs of the ongoing business. A formal selection process, often including outside advisors, can be used to help the owners handle a decision that has the potential to seriously damage family relationships if done arbitrarily by the parents or through an arbitrary decision-making process.

### #2 – I Need to Protect My Major Source of Income

For many founders the business is their major source of income and they feel the need to protect it. Handing control to the next generation feels like permitting the children to manage their retirement investment portfolios. Unfortunately many business owners have not diversified their equity, having put everything they earned back into the family operation. The danger of operating in this fashion is more clearly seen during the succession planning and retirement process when it hinders many of them from transferring the necessary control and power—the most difficult elements of the business to transfer—to the next generation. Having all their equity in the business seems to increase the risk factor for founders at an age when they tend to be much more risk-averse.

### #1 – What If the Next Generation Does Better?

One of the most profound reasons for the reluctance founders demonstrate in giving up control is the often unconscious fear that the next generation may run the business better than they have. It is indeed a paradoxical fear of being diminished by the success of one's offspring. This age-old pattern dates back to antiquity, where the king would sometimes kill his oldest son because he was too much of a threat to the throne. Unfortunately, founders who function as monarchs can easily find ways to stifle and hinder the progress and development of their offspring. The easiest way for them to "kill" their children is to avoid engaging in any succession planning. Refusing to do so when the children are beyond thirty-five years of age is essentially a way of trapping them in the family business. The underlying message being sent is that the parents plan to control them forever through the family firm. Something vital dies within the children at that point, and the "founderitis" virus will have accomplished its mission by destroying what is most important to the founder—the individual health and vitality of the family.

### Healthy Retirement: A New Model for Aging

*At age 97, George Burns was asked, "What does your doctor say about your smoking and your drinking? Burns, in his wry comedic style, replied, "My doctor is dead."*

At the heart of "founderitis" is our fear of aging and all the myths and misperceptions associated with the process of normal human development. And what has been perceived as normal and fairly inevitable, at least in popular culture, is that after approximately the age of forty, our toboggan starts sliding down the other side of the hill. Our bodies begin to deteriorate and our mental capacity and performance begins its inevitable journey into the declining sunset. I am going to suggest that there is a very different way to understand the normal human aging process. And with that new understanding comes the opportunity to embrace healthy aging and develop a healthy retirement strategy.

### *"Use It or Lose It": It's All in Your Brain*

The brain can change itself! "Neuroplasticity" is the term coined by scientists to refer to this revolutionary discovery, which overthrows the centuries-old belief that the adult brain is hard-wired, fixed and unchanging.[1] According to Dr. George Vaillant, a psychiatrist who heads up the Harvard Study of Adult Development, old age is not simply a process of inevitable decline and decay. After tracking people for over six decades, he concludes that older people often develop new skills and are often wiser than they were in younger years. In addition, the elderly can be less prone to depression than younger people (Doidge, p. 256). And the consensus among scholars is that when it comes to human creativity, people between 35 and 55 are at their peak in most fields. Moreover, research shows that although people in their sixties and seventies work at a slower pace, they can be just as productive as in their twenties.[2]

Motivation is clearly a key factor in our ability to exercise the brain. Instead of viewing retirement as "the end of the road" and allowing negative thinking to become a self-fulfilling prophecy that accelerates our mental decline, we need to heed neuroscientific research demonstrating that we actually have a "use-it-or-lose-it" brain. Examples abound. Nelson Mandela was seventy when he was released from prison and led the drive to free South Africa from apartheid. Laura Ingalls Wilder first published *Little House on the Prairie* at age sixty-eight and then went on to finish the entire series of books about her life at age seventy-five. Martha Graham danced until her mid-seventies and continued to choreograph for another twenty-one years, choreographing her final dance at the age of ninety-six. The famous architect Frank Lloyd Wright designed the Guggenheim Museum at age ninety. When Pablo Casals, the renowned cellist, at age ninety was asked, "Why do you continue to practice?" Casals replied, "Because I am making progress."

We need a new model of aging that can help us both understand and fully optimize our own capacity for change. There might not be a cure for "founderitis," but there are signposts of hope, the first being our understanding of the power to change that resides in our brain. The second is a reformulation of human development during the second half of life—a topic only recently being given much attention. In summary, our brains have the inherent capacity to change and to grow throughout the entire cycle of life. And just as important, our genes, expressed through brain functioning, can be altered by experience. These capabilities have two massive implications for the aging process. Firstly, our brain is wired so that if we don't use it, we will lose its full potential. Secondly, and more positively, we have the capacity to continually train the brain or to re-sculpt our dendrites and synapses in order to increase brain functioning capacity throughout our entire lifespan.

### Understanding the Second Half of Your Life

Four sequential but overlapping phases of later life have been identified by Dr. Gene Cohen (see the chart on page 94).[3] These phases are based on qualitative research and an extensive interview process and they are noteworthy and groundbreaking because they provide a dynamic model of aging based upon our creative potential and capacity for change. And these phases are premised upon a more extensive and recent understanding both of human brain functioning and human brain potential.

## What to Do with the
## Second Half of Your Life
## (Sequential and Overlapping Phases)

### *Mid-life Re-evaluation (35–65)*
#### (*Ambivalence*)

- Where have I been?
- Where am I now?
- Where am I going?

### *Liberation (50–75)*
#### (*Freedom to do the right thing*)

- Desire to experiment and innovate
- "If not now—when?"
- "What can they do to me?"

### *Summing Up (60–100)*
#### (*Linking heart and mind*)

- Recap—autobiographic writing
- Resolve—outstanding conflicts, issues
- Contribute—volunteerism, philanthropy

### *Encore (65–100+)*
#### (*Continue creativity*)

- Reflection
- Desire for continuation
- Celebration

### 1. Mid-life Re-evaluation Phase (35–65)

Contrary to some popular literature and previously held theories, only about 10% of people have an actual mid-life crisis. Much more significant is the reality that most of us go through a mid-life re-evaluation sometime between the ages of 35 and 65. During this time we tend to ask ourselves some form of the following questions: Where have I been? Where am I now? Where am I going? This period marks the onset of greater reflection about how much time we have left as opposed to the time already lived. It is a time of ambivalence: a phase in our maturation during which we attempt to hold competing issues and solutions in a healthy balance. Someone has joked that men go through mid-life re-evaluation at age thirty-nine, at age forty-nine, at age fifty-nine, and so on. During these times founders who are contemplating major business transitions can find themselves confusing their personal re-evaluations with their strategic business challenges.

### 2. Liberation Phase (50–75)

Being able to resolve one's personal re-evaluation phase(s) usually leads us into a time of great freedom. This phase is dominated by the desire to experiment and to innovate. It is a time of life when you often hear people saying "If not now, then when?" or "I've got nothing to lose." It can be a period of great authenticity and personal honesty, particularly if one's re-evaluation has been thorough. Interestingly, research shows that the time between ages fifty and eighty is the stage of our life cycle in which we have the largest number of dendrites in the hippocampus part of the brain. For us non-scientists, that indicates tremendous capacity to process information. Founders who are truly liberated also possess great internal power. Their ability to influence family and business events and transactions increases commensurate with their ability to resolve and balance the disparate tensions and demands within their own life. They have truly earned the right to teach (but not to "preach," as I warned one founder who

quite enjoyed occupying the bully pulpit with his family). Mark
Twain, on his seventieth birthday, perhaps summed it up best:
"The seventieth birthday! It is the time of life when you arrive at
a new and awful dignity; when you may throw aside the decent
reserves which have oppressed you for a generation and stand un-
afraid and unabashed upon your seven-terraced summit and look
down and teach—unrebuked" (Cohen, p. 10).

### 3. Summing-Up Phase (60–100)

This phase can best be characterized as a desire to give back and
follows times of liberation. During this time we review our life, we
resolve outstanding conflicts, and we engage in making social con-
tributions. We give back in a variety of ways. Many people write
their memoirs during this time of life—expressing their desire to
leave a historical legacy for subsequent generations. My own parents both finished writing their memoirs last year while in their
early eighties. Their writing was clearly an exercise in punctuating
or summing up their memorable and unique life stories. But their
stated goal was always to leave their story for their grandchildren
so that it would not be lost and forgotten.

Volunteering and philanthropy, which tends to be strong among
persons into their eighties, is essentially a summing-up activity. It
is also during this time that we attempt to tie up loose ends—particularly in our relational life. Renewed and sincere efforts to resolve long-standing conflicts among close friends and family members are common during this phase.

Research into brain activity contributes to our understanding
of the summing-up period. Studies indicate that as they age, older people actually harness both sides of the brain to a much greater extent than younger persons. Whether this is compensatory
brain function or new-found capacity is under study—but the
conclusion to be drawn is that the brain has the capacity to mod-
ify its functioning by recruiting other areas of the brain. We actually have a greater capacity to take care of unfinished business

as we age because heart and mind, left and right brain, are linking up in new ways.

In effect, as we age we use the whole brain more (Cohen, p. 11).

### 4. Encore Phase (65–100+)

As we age, the desire to reflect upon our life and to celebrate our achievements represents an innate drive for continuity. Ancients referred to this impulse as the quest for immortality. Why not an encore to a life well lived? Birthdays are often celebrated with greater poignancy later in life, and anniversaries take on more profound meaning. And despite physical limitations for some during our later years, our mind continues its inexorable journey to express itself through creative and well-developed habits of thought and behaviour. To continue with our life's achievement—to do it one more time—to walk the acreage we have spent a lifetime harvesting—to do one more business deal and feel the buzz—to have another encore. We need encores and we continue to seek them. In another more agrarian era we talked about this phase as "going with our boots on." I think of a grandfather who continued producing and generating musical commissions into his eighties. His many encores surprised friends and colleagues, and he was considered far more innovative than many members of the younger generations who followed him. Dr. Gene Cohen, past president of the Gerontological Society of America, recounts the following:

> Dear Abby once asked a 105-year-old woman what the advantages of being a centenarian were. The woman reflected for a moment, then replied, "There's less peer pressure."

### Ten Ways to Challenge Your Mind and Improve Your Health as You Age[4]

1. **Challenge your mind.** Play more games and do puzzles—you can increase your vocabulary into your eighties.

2. **Entertain and discuss.** Engage in provocative discussions and stimulating friendships.

3. **Travel and explore.** This can be a city museum or a new international destination.

4. **Enrol in an educational course.** Elderhostel is a good example of life-long learning; other courses provide intergenerational experiences.

5. **Explore a new hobby or craft.** Visit the bookstore for ideas.

6. **Volunteer.** Among those aged 75+, nearly 40% continue to volunteer.

7. **Start a new business or a new career.** Fulfill that entrepreneurial itch; attitudes toward older workers have vastly improved.

8. **Write more letters and e-mails.** Grandkids are the best at returning e-mails.

9. **Keep a journal.** Write down your dreams and thoughts; draw pictures; tap into your creative side.

10. **Write your memoirs or family history.**

# CHAPTER 8

## *SOBS (SONS OF BOSSES)*

*"A man is not a man until his father tells him he is a man."*
*– Anonymous*

Fathers and their sons—a relationship that dominates many family businesses and yet is so little understood. In 1992, John Thies and Peter Naus, two psychologists at the University of Waterloo, researched the relationship between men and their sexuality, trying to understand what made them unique both in perspective and in practice. Without labelling or judging, and through a significantly large interview process, they sought to determine the differences between men's and women's approaches to sexuality and intimacy. Throughout the study a single issue kept emerging, particularly for men with what they termed dysfunctional sexuality and intimacy issues (such as affairs, sexual performance issues, multiple divorces or sexual abuse). That common factor was the father-son relationship. Their conclusion, supported by most research on the topic, was that male capacity for healthy and satisfying intimacy and men's ability to be confident in relationships in general stemmed primarily from their own relationships with their fathers.[1]

The history of father-son relationships is fraught with difficulties. In the film *Dead Poets Society*, Robin Williams plays an English teacher at a prestigious prep school. As an award-winning educator, he succeeds in exciting his students about literature and the reading of classic poetry. One of his outstanding students is a boy of seventeen who develops a passion for drama and acting. He wins a lead role in the school play and delivers an exceptional performance. However, his father, a corporate executive from Philadelphia, has plans for his son to become a lawyer, climb the corporate ladder and move onto Wall Street. The last thing he wants is for his son to waste time memorizing lines for the school play.

Unbeknown to the son, the father shows up for the last performance. As he watches his son, we see the colour rise in his face. He becomes livid with anger, furious that his son has deviated from the prescribed course of study without permission. The outcome is tragic. The father drags his son from the theatre by the ear and drives him home in complete humiliation. The next day the son takes his own life in his father's office. The scene can be viewed as a tragic conclusion to a father's projected succession plan.

The movie *Gladiator* is another family business story, only this time the family is the Caesars and the business is the Roman Empire. Caesar realizes that he is getting old and needs to make a decision concerning succession. He decides that his successor will be his top general (played in this movie by Russell Crowe) and communicates the choice to him. Then he faces the task of informing his own son about a succession choice that does not involve nepotism. The encounter is a dramatic scene that sets up the conflict for the rest of the movie. Caesar invites his son into his tent and essentially tells him "Look, son, I sort of like you, but basically you don't have the goods to run the Empire." Caesar's son listens to this lack of affirmation, to this indictment of his worthiness, and we see the muscles tighten in his neck and jaw. We can imagine what it must feel like to be told by your father that you don't have what it takes. And what does this son do? He initially attempts to argue his case: "Wait a minute, Dad. I might not have all the qualities that you are looking for, but I've got other qualities. I've got ambition, I'm a good negotiator, I am devious, I am treacherous ..." However, he senses that all his pleadings are to no avail. Then the grisly moment occurs. The son kills his father and widespread conflict ensues.

These two movies, *Dead Poets Society* and *Gladiator*, reflect the extremes that can exist within a father-son relationship. What is it about this relationship that causes such polarized reactions?

From the beginning of time relationships between fathers and sons have been problematic. As fathers, our hearts ache with love, anticipation and excitement for our children when they are born. We would do anything to nurture and ensure a bright and productive future for our young children. Then, all too soon, they become teenagers and begin to exhibit attitudes and behaviour that

> **"Some psychologists say that a dad is the single most important element in the formation of a child's character."**

try our patience to the utmost. All of us, parents and children, harbour metaphorical thoughts of wanting to strangle the other. We can quickly move into encounters in which a son can break our hearts or we can break his. One family business owner who had a very troubled relationship with one of his children showed me a Father's Day card that he had received from his son. It read as follows: "Some psychologists say that a dad is the single most important element in the formation of a child's character. In other words, I'm mostly your fault." The father turned to me and commented, "At least I got a card."

### My Father's Blessing

When I was nineteen years old, having finished one year of university, I decided that I wanted to head west and travel around the world to find my own fame and fortune. I packed all my worldly belongings into my car and planned to go wherever the road took me. This is what you do when you are nineteen and essentially lost. Since my parents really didn't know when they would see me next, my father followed me in his car to the junction of the highway that was to lead me westward. At the junction we stopped our vehicles and both of us got out. I will never forget this moment. My dad was a man of very few words and not accustomed to expressing his feelings very well, if at all. He turned to me and asked, "John, is there anything between us?" And I replied, "No, Dad." Then we gave each other a big hug and, as far as I remember, this was the first time I ever saw him cry. He told me he was proud of me and he wished me well on my journey.

My dad had given me his blessing. It was something that I had always felt intuitively, but this was the first time he had actually spoken it. His blessing was all that I needed as I left home, in my mind perhaps never to return again. My parents, now both in their eighties, live within blocks of our house, and there isn't a week when I don't drop over and give my dad a big hug and tell him that I love him. I believe that my dad laid a foundation for this family harmony when I was a nineteen-year-old searching for my identity. My father gave me the most precious gift that a young man can receive when he is trying to transition into adulthood—his blessing. By "blessing," I simply mean the assurance that you are appreciated and respected. My dad showed me that he believed and trusted in my fundamental goodness. I believe that every child needs this.

If researchers determine that father-son relationships are difficult at the best of times, imagine the extra layers of problems among SOBs (sons of bosses). The following SOB scenarios highlight the sorts of puzzling and sometimes troubling relationships that sons and their fathers live through.

### Raising Cain

One of the oldest family business stories in recorded history is also one of the first stories in the Hebrew Bible. Cain and Abel are brothers managing a large farming operation. Cain handles the crops, and Abel the livestock. Their father happens to have more interest in cattle than in crops. This results in his spending a lot more time with his son Abel than he does with Cain. Cain is sensitive and also jealous and begins to feel slighted. He perceives that Dad is making deals with Abel that will eventually result in the phasing out of crops. Perhaps he will even lose his inheritance. At a very deep level Cain doesn't feel respected or understood by his father. How could he when his dad is not spending any quality time with him? This troubling relationship leads to a scenario that is very familiar to all of us. A poor sense of self-worth prompts hatred of a brother, and we know where hatred leads. Cain ends up killing Abel.

My guess is that Dad probably didn't know how his sons were feeling towards each other. Did he take the time to ask them? Did the father show approval to his sons? How did he affirm his two farm boys? Fratricide does not take place in a vacuum.

In my work with next-generation males between the ages of eighteen and thirty-five, I have witnessed many who exhibit what I call a wound. The wound is in the shape of a hollowed-out sense of self-worth resulting from a troubled relationship with their father. As described in the study on male intimacy by Thies and Naus, all of the men who had had affairs also commented that their fathers had never been affirming. They had never received their father's blessing. In the story of Cain and Abel, Cain's perception of favouritism and the absence of his father's appreciation led to the murder of his brother. There are many ways to hurt or kill your children—the easiest is simply to withhold affirmation and praise. And for maximum effect, start that pattern of non-approval very early. If your children survive, they will most likely do so with severe issues of inadequacy.

### An Invisible Daughter

Daughters also need their father's blessing. I worked with a father who is one of the largest producers in his agricultural sector. He knows to the last penny what his fuel costs are, what his labour and veterinary costs are, and all the inputs contributing to the successful management of his two-thousand-acre farm. This quality control expert has every fact pertinent to the successful running of his agribusiness under control. However, he has no idea what his eldest daughter thinks about the operation and how she feels about her relationships with her father, mother and brothers. She and her own family no longer attend extended family gatherings because the relationship between her and her father is almost irreparably damaged. Constantly fighting back tears of frustration and rage, she is verbally prepared to kill one of her brothers, whom she views as Dad's favourite. Dad seems completely unaware and has no ability to affirm any of his children. None of them has received his blessing. Is it any wonder that this business family finds succession planning impossible to complete?

### Shotgun Clause vs. Genuine Choices

Uncle Abe and Larry, his nephew, were running a huge ranching operation with cattle and sheep in a very lush valley. However, growth was limited by the size of the valley. Uncle Abe was quite a bit older than his relative and had more power due both to his age and his equity position. He also knew the contents of the shareholder agreement intimately because he had written it. He could easily have invoked the buy-sell clause and said to his young nephew, "Larry, I'm taking over and buying you out. You're out of this operation." Instead, he took Larry to the local tavern and the two men sat down. The uncle told Larry that he had several choices. The first was to stay and take half the livestock. Since this was a fixed operation, it would not be able to grow. On the other hand, there would be no risk and Larry would be very comfortable. Option number two was to take half the livestock and find another valley. Uncle Abe was prepared to let Larry have first choice of valleys. Larry, who was comfortable where he was, chose this option, but decided to stay put. So Uncle Abe—the Old Testament patriarch Abraham—gathered his half of the livestock and travelled to what became the Promised Land, where he grew wealthy. His people are still going strong today. Larry (Lot in the Biblical story) remained in the original valley and ran the fixed operation without any risk. He invested in the local Sodom stock market. Eventually it collapsed and he lost all his wealth.

This story is really about the provision of genuine options. All too often the next-generation members of business families feel that they do not have genuine choices. The family business wraps its benevolent arms around them whether they like it or not. Perhaps they would have liked to go to school. Maybe they would have preferred to become a pilot, but the only permissible course was to work in the family business. Not so in this tale. Larry was given real options, although he didn't necessarily choose wisely.

For children in business families, this story poses four salient questions:

1. Do you feel you had a genuine choice as to whether or not to enter the family business?
2. Do you feel you have a genuine option to leave the family business?
3. Do you have genuine choices as to the nature of your involvement with and the direction of the family business?
4. Do you have the freedom to fail?

### Anointing the "Favourite Son"

Isaac was in his eighties and finally ready to sign off on the succession documents. He had his will prepared, as well as the deed to the key land holdings which drove the business. As was the custom, his intention was to pass operational control of the business to his oldest son, Esau. However, the complications of a blended family interfered, as his wife favoured her own son, Jacob. She had consulted with an independent counsel and had managed to slip in an altered legal document without Isaac's knowledge at the last minute. This, in combination with the manipulation of some shareholder options, allowed Jacob to gain legal control of the family empire. Thus began a long journey of estrangement. Esau and Jacob finally sorted out their business differences, but the family never again functioned as a proper cohesive unit.

Jacob learned his lesson. He was determined not to wait as long as his father to implement a succession plan. Although he had twelve sons, he quickly picked a favourite: son number eleven, named Joseph. Joseph was intelligent, very good-looking and a natural leader. However, the other brothers were livid, many consumed with jealousy and anger. Were they consulted or even considered? Where was the impartial and formal process of decision-making? What were the criteria for leadership? After this arbitrary decision the boys realized that their father couldn't be taken seriously and he thus became irrelevant to them. They quickly took care of the matter by selling their brother Joseph into slavery.

This familiar story has been popularized by the famous musical *Joseph and the Amazing Technicolor Dreamcoat*. In the long run, maybe Dad did make the right choice. However, the lack of a more formal and less arbitrary process of decision-making destroyed Jacob's family and eventually the family business. Dad's favouritism did Joseph no favours either. Choosing a next-generation leader from among the children is one of the most difficult decisions for parents. As this story shows, the repercussions of not taking one's time in the decision-making process can be extremely damaging.

### You Can't Fire Me: I'm Your Dad[2]

David was president of a very large and successful empire. His favourite son from his second marriage had just turned thirty. Abbey was smart, spoiled and hugely ambitious. His dad had already given him half of the company divisions to manage, but Abbey sensed a ceiling to his future promotions. Dad was still quite young and vigorous and wasn't likely to give up control of the business for at least another twenty years. Surreptitiously Abbey began to line up

> *"There are two golden rules in life. When violated, they often result in personal and business ruin. The first is 'Treat others as you yourself wish to be treated.' The second is 'Whoever has the gold makes the rules.'"*

his troops. His father responded with surprising passivity. Abbey interpreted his father's response as capitulation and surrender. In reality, Dad was beside himself with grief. He could not believe that his favourite son would betray him. Abbey attacked, but in his youthful haste and greed he had not done his homework. His unfriendly takeover attempt was quickly thwarted by his father's legal and accounting team. During the affair, the son's illegal manoeuvres came to light. There was a prison sentence, and Abbey died of a drug overdose a month later. His father was never the same after this episode. He lost both his joy for living and his competitive, entrepreneurial edge. The family business had reached its peak and started a slow but lengthy decline.

There are two golden rules in life. When violated, they often result in personal and business ruin. The first is "Treat others as you yourself wish to be treated." The second is "Whoever has the gold makes the rules."

The first aphorism is the universal rule of reciprocity, which is the foundation of all ethical formulations, moral behaviour and family values. The second is a proverb that identifies the practical and functional reality of power relationships. In the preceding story (a retelling of the biblical story of King David and his son Absalom), Abbey gave no indication of understanding, let alone acting on, either of these universal rules. As a next-generation son of the boss, his unbridled aggression in seeking to wrest control from his father provided a stark and unfavourable contrast to his father's kindness and generosity.

## Fair vs. Equal

There were once two sons. The youngest son, Chip, was fed up with the family business and demanded an early inheritance from his father. He wanted to seek fame and fortune elsewhere. Since he had worked in the family business for some time, his father complied, providing him with funds for his venture. Chip spent the next three years living in the fast lane—Caribbean beaches, many women, too many drugs and too many bad trips. Finally, destitute, sick and out of money, Chip, a.k.a. the prodigal son, came to his senses and called his father to ask if there might be a chance for him to return to the family business. Dad was overjoyed. Not only did he throw a huge welcoming party, but he also reinstated Chip within the firm's ownership structure, gifting him with significant ownership shares. Chip's older brother, who had faithfully soldiered on in a top management position during the three years in which Chip sowed his wild oats, was completely outraged. To begin with, he considered it improper for Chip to receive company shares. Not only were they undeserved, but the value of his own ownership shares was diluted. Secondly, he simply didn't trust his younger brother, given his past history of irresponsibility. Thirdly, he was very angry with his father because he had not been consulted in any of these matters, which had a bearing on the future strategic direction of the company and any succession planning involving him.

The father, in his haste to forgive Chip and reinstate his youngest son on an equal footing within the family business, had unconsciously violated a significant principle. Life is not always fair, and people are not created equal. Furthermore, within family business environments, fairness does not usually signify equality. Like many owners before him, this father had the family and the business confused. Most parents attempt to treat their children equally when doing their estate planning. This is normal and reflects best practices. However, it is not a best practice to treat family members equally within the business. The bottom line in business is competence, productivity and profit. Transferring the family business to one or a combination of next-generation family members needs to happen within the framework of a legitimate and fair business transaction. Best practices would indicate that next-generation members involved in the business be paid and be able to purchase the business from the parents/estate on the basis of their competence and potential for successful future leadership. Best practices as a rule would indicate that family members who are not active in business operations should not be gifted nor allowed to purchase shares in the family business. Such a practice could be seen as unfair by the family members driving the business operations.

### The Zero Sum Game

In John Updike's novels *Rabbit is Rich* and *Rabbit at Rest*,[3] the father (Rabbit) is a middle-aged man who inherits a Toyota dealership and feels trapped. His son Nelson, who is in his early twenties and craves his father's love and approval, returns home after a year at university and asks to participate in the family business. Initially Rabbit is unwilling to allow him in, primarily because of his own deep feelings of insecurity. As a result, he is unable to meet his son's needs and in fact undermines Nelson by dismissing his suggestions about the business. Ten years later, Rabbit is still unwilling to let go and by now displays open contempt for his son. Nelson has fallen into a predictable pattern of feeling trapped within the family business, and although Dad feels partly responsible for his son's drug habit, he still cannot bring himself to share control of the business.

This is another sad tale of a father and son who seem to have no regard for each other. Unfortunately, the younger generation is always the most vulnerable in these situations. The son's success is threatening to the father and thus Rabbit refuses to transfer any real authority and control to Nelson. Rabbit himself is trying to escape from the snare of the inherited Toyota dealership. Because of this he unwittingly undermines his son's self-confidence, eventually prompting his unfortunate demise.

This story reflects paradoxical underlying emotional issues. Most fathers promote their sons' achievements because "a successful son reflects a successful father." However, if the son surpasses the father, then he runs the risk of shaming his father. Sons learn the meaning of "being a man" first of all by engaging with their own fathers. They need approval, mentoring and appropriate modelling in order to absorb the "meaning of manhood." Unfortunately, many sons within business families receive only criticism, benign neglect from workaholic dads and very little actual modelling of a healthy male role in society or business.

Updike's tale also reveals the ironic paradox of SOBs attempting to become adults. On the one hand, adulthood requires independence and self-responsibility. However, working within the family business context too often prolongs the dependence of the next generation. If this tension is not resolved constructively by the age of thirty-five or forty, the son invariably moves into mid-life crisis mode. The inability to resolve identity issues—that is, the failure to find his genuine voice within the family business system—invariably leads the son to feel he has a limited number of genuine choices. Too often his sense of being trapped within the family business leads him to choose escape patterns that end up as destructive addictions, rather than moving into the future with a sense of responsibility for his choices and actions. Nelson exhibits this classic SOB pattern in his struggle to achieve independence within his father's company and in his subsequent descent into drug addiction.

### Conclusion

Variations of these six SOB scenarios occur daily in family firms:

1. Lack of mutual affirmation.
2. Difficulty in making genuine choices.
3. Favouritism and lack of formal succession processes.
4. Power struggles.

5. Confusion of fair and equal treatment in dealing with the next generation.
6. The zero sum game reflecting lack of self-esteem and self-worth.

The implications of father-son interactions during succession planning would indicate that the problematic periods in a young man's life are his twenties and forties, both of which are decades of intense identity formation and re-evaluation. In his thirties, a son tends to experience a calmer time, and thus this period offers more harmonious possibilities for discussing succession planning. Regardless of one's life stage, the three most problematic periods for father-son relationships are during the successor's initial entry into the family business; during the succession planning process; and during the founder's contemplation of retirement.

# CHAPTER 9

# MALE MENOPAUSE: THE HIDDEN FEAR

*"I know what men want. Men want to be really, really close to someone who will leave them alone."* – Elayne Boosler

In an August 2002 *Harvard Gazette* article entitled "Marriage Lowers Testosterone," the question was asked: "If testosterone levels flatten out at age sixty, does that mean males undergo a menopause?"[1] Not according to the scientists. "Male testosterone lessens with age but there's no discrete end. No cliff that falls off as when women use up their finite supply of eggs." One physician puts it this way: "Men … don't have menses to pause."

On the subject of testosterone, Jay Leno of the *Tonight Show* commented on a study reporting that overly competitive people—people who constantly disrupt conversations and always have to prove that they are right—tend to die younger. Quipped Leno, "Scientists call these people men."

During a CBC documentary on the same topic, the term "andropause" was coined to describe a more comprehensive assortment of changes that accompanies a life stage for men that is finding much more air time than at any previous point in history. The fact that erectile dysfunction has entered everyday conversation and the ubiquitous presence of advertising for Viagra, Cialis, etc., on television and the Internet points to an underlying reality that also has implications for entrepreneurial founders.

Two Harvard researchers, Gray and Ellison, take note of what they call a "silent experiment" that is taking place. They maintain that scientists have been manipulating testosterone levels in men to see what happens. They claim that this manipulation is unethical, yet "physicians wrote more than a million prescriptions for the hormone testosterone in 2001 for men who hope that it will raise their libido, slow aging, and reduce muscle and bone loss. No scientific study has conclusively demonstrated that these results will actually occur, but demand is high for testosterone patches and Androgel, a salve that men rub on their skin."[2]

So who is afraid of male menopause? Or Andropause? Or the inevitable and normal aging process of current baby boomers? I believe the answer is many more than would care to admit it publicly. And I believe that this holds true particularly among men. Otherwise we as males would have been discussing this matter a long time ago and in a much more open manner.

Very often the precursor to a man's mid-life crisis is certain actual signs of change and the perception that "the toboggan is starting to go down the other side of the hill." For men, these perceptions often trigger a variety of hard-to-manage emotions. The central issue for many males is the sense of being in control. Men quite enjoy being in control—of their businesses, their inventions, their families, their destinies. When they are confronted with the obstacles of life and the inevitability of the aging process, including the drop in testosterone, they realize with a huge gasp that—wow—they are not completely in control of this thing. Something is happening that seems to have a life of its own and they can't control it. For family business leaders who are used to directing businesses and economic empires of their own creation, the emotions related to this loss of control are difficult to understand, categorize and manage. The central issue is change and how we cope with change.

The signs of change can take many forms. We glance in the mirror one morning as we are blow-drying our hair and realize that it's not taking us as long and that the pink patch at the top of our forehead seems more pronounced; we enter our next board meeting with a slightly more hesitant step. Some of us have to upgrade our eyeglass prescriptions in order to read the newspaper and then quickly get laser surgery done in order not to have to admit to our peers, clients and friends that we are now over forty. Our chests start feeling tight and we are perpetually twenty-five pounds over our ideal weight. We avoid climbing stairs. We avoid telling our wives about our ailments and won't go see a doctor because we are afraid of what the doctor will tell us; we might be admonished to actually change some habits. While playing in that pick-up hockey league we begin to realize that we have lost a few steps because we just can't catch those younger old-timers (between forty and fifty) as they beat us to the goalie. And it is taking us more than just a day to recover from the aches and bruises.

How many times have we as men faked being asleep when our wives get into bed with that gleam in their eyes? The nature of men's sexual performance also changes. It is a biological fact that most men don't perform sexually at age fifty in quite the same way as they did at age nineteen. Yet it is surprising how many men are embarrassed to the point of being ashamed of this phenomenon. Rather than discussing these changes openly, many men would rather shy away from further intimacy. The longer the problem is not discussed between couples, the bigger it gets. One day an elephant shows up in the bedroom. Husband and wife move into separate beds, eventually into separate rooms, and ultimately they begin to lead separate lives.

At a purely biological level, andropause is simply about getting older. But more importantly, andropause is about a larger challenge to a man's view of himself. It encompasses the totality of physical, hormonal, psychological and relational phenomena trendily referred to as "male menopause." In contrast to menopause, a normalized transition that now occurs within relative silence, male menopause still seems to be a taboo subject among men, probably because it is a phenomenon that strikes at the core of male identity. Just as menopause signals the end of a woman's fertility, male menopause signals changes in a man's virility. Note carefully: not necessarily a loss of virility—but often significant changes. His youthful sexual drive and performance—the source of his fantasies—and what he has counted on to bring him pleasure seems to be at stake. And that can scare the stuffing out of men.

In our businesses we can control most of the changes that come along. We can often predict the changes that are coming along. We can act proactively to flex with these changes. We can actually be initiators of the change processes necessary for our businesses to grow and thrive. And healthy and mature business leaders guide changes such as the "succession process."

However, many men, including family business leaders who are facing andropause—whether that is experienced physically, emotionally or relationally—feel a loss of control. When that occurs, a common response is to tighten control in other areas of life. So instead of welcoming a natural stage of life and growing through it by embracing it, many men perceive it as a time of loss and redouble their efforts to make sure that they don't lose anything else. And for many family business entrepreneurs, that "anything else" is often their unchallenged control over their business. Their difficulty in handling change more creatively can become a major factor in their inability to accept, let alone initiate and manage, the succession process. The entire "succession scenario" can be just another emotional signpost of their inevitable loss of control.

Unlike women, men may not view change as an opportunity for growth. Instead, they often associate change with loss, the giving up of power, being overtaken by the younger generation. Some even see change as failure. Change isn't necessarily viewed as a positive ingredient of inner growth and freedom. Particularly during the first half of their lives, men are rewarded for focusing almost single-

> **"A man's identity is often tied up with the status he has achieved in his thirties, forties and fifties."**

mindedly on the pursuit of a successful career path and/or the building of their businesses. Life seems straightforward and simple. When their career path takes an abrupt turn, the demands of the business change, their physical energy diminishes, and their offspring want to take over the family firm, many men face a crisis of meaning. Even though they are floundering during such times of acute transition, men are stereotypically reluctant to ask for help. They haven't been taught to ask questions about their sexual life cycle, their physical health or their psychological well-being.

The workplace and the nature of our businesses are also characterized by constant flux. Within our high-technology world, experience may not be as valued as it once was. Men are forced to adapt to changing economic environments and even to make complete career shifts at an increasing pace. As family businesses grow and marketplace competition heats up, the CEOs become younger, organizations have to professionalize in order to remain competitive, and competent next-generation members are faced with increasingly attractive opportunities outside their own family firms.

Women seem to adapt to the changes of mid-life with less angst. They may feel pangs at the loss of their youth, but men often describe the process with dread. Mid-life men have concerns about aging and the ebbing of physical strength and athletic prowess, fears around job security and the loss of their own aging fathers, desires to be closer to their children before they lose them, pre-retirement anxieties, and the bigger question of potency in all areas of their lives. A man's identity is often tied up with the status he has achieved in his thirties, forties and fifties. If he slows down and relaxes even a little bit, will that status slip away?

Men may feel stuck or even trapped by their financial responsibilities. Men's linear thinking may lead them to believe that the achievement of material prosperity will make them happy. But their material accomplishments may fail to provide meaning and joy as expected. Men can become frustrated, angry, confused, scared and ashamed to admit any of these emotions.

Transitional periods like pre-retirement can be unsettling for everyone. But a lack of awareness during this time can make it even more difficult. Denial leading to depression and self-destructive behaviour is more likely to occur if middle life isn't approached with knowledge and an open mind.

Gail Sheehy, in her book *Understanding Men's Passages,*[3] argues that the middle years are the stage of potentially highest well-being in the lives of healthy educated people and explores the concept of "second adulthood." This is a way of viewing the years from forty to ninety as an opportunity to redefine fulfillment and counteract fear of retirement and "founderitis."

### *Facing the Mid-Life Authenticity Crisis: From Competing to Connecting*

Men actually have the same primary needs for closeness, connectedness and intimacy as women, only they have a more difficult time acknowledging those needs. That difficulty causes men to pull away from intimacy when sexual habits or performance change with age. This can lead some men to desperately hang on to power in other areas of their lives, particularly in their business roles and in their role as family leader. Family business founders are therefore vulnerable to succession difficulties because of their drive for power and control in both spheres. We previously coined the term "founderitis" to characterize this threat to their mid-life authenticity.

"How can I get my husband to open up and talk about his feelings, or just talk?" is a frequently articulated question during family business workshops. Many wives then go on to describe how their husband's embarrassment and shame have led to a shutdown of commu-

> *"Men who achieve a healthy balance between competing and connecting are those who exercise regularly, practice good nutrition, adopt a generally healthy lifestyle, and cultivate closer friendships with their mates and other friends. These preventive habits are the key to minimizing the adverse effects of aging and stress on male potency."*

nication with their partner. The source of embarrassment and shame varies. We have already described some of the physical changes and the perceptions of inadequacy that result. For some men it is their sense that they are not providing adequately for their families. Some personalize a business failure, seeing it as the result of their own defects or incompetent decision-making. Others perceive strained relations with their children as lack of respect for their authority and personalize the next generation's need for independence as rejection. For many men the resulting marital and family discord wreaks havoc with sound business and succession planning.

The challenge is to open up an authentic dialogue around these fears of aging and interpretive perceptions of changes in family relations without making the problem worse. Achieving new definitions of business family success and marital intimacy depends upon these initially difficult conversations. Although withdrawing and stonewalling are some of the defence mechanisms used by men who are threatened by the combination of physical and relational changes, their basic need for human closeness and intimacy actually becomes more persistent as they grow older. Men who achieve a healthy balance between competing and connecting are those who exercise regularly, practice good nutrition, adopt a generally healthy lifestyle, and cultivate closer friendships with their mates

> *"Family business members are prone to the most socially acceptable form of addictive behaviour, namely, work. Much of this addictive behaviour, whether alcoholism or workaholism, is actually disguised depression."*

and other friends. These preventive habits are the key to minimizing the adverse effects of aging and stress on male potency.

The father-son relationship can also become the arena for a mid-life power struggle. A grown-up son has the potential to make his father feel redundant, particularly if they share the same workplace. The father has the need to feel that "I can still do it—I'm the man!" The son on the other hand wants his father to see him as an adult with the full capabilities of manhood, and not as a little boy. So fathers and sons engage in the dance of male intimacy. Sons may be embarrassed to admit their mistakes to their fathers, yet still want their praise, affirmation and respect. Fathers actually learn to connect best through being close to their children. Yet they may find it wrenching to recognize their son's need to move towards greater independence in order to become a healthy adult.

All leading family therapists encourage men to heal the father-son relationship sooner rather than later. For if a father dies abruptly, before a son feels ready to assume the role as head of the family and possibly the family business, the result can be a long and rocky mid-life passage for the son. The term "mid-life delinquent" has been coined to describe middle-aged men who exhibit addictive behaviours that extend beyond alcohol and drugs to include food and sexual addictions. ("It's a little like white-collar crime—it's taking place but it's hidden.")[4] Family business members are prone to the most socially acceptable form of addictive behaviour, namely *work*. Much of this addictive behaviour, whether alcoholism or workaholism, is actually disguised depression. Men in mid-life transition are attempting to retain a sense of personal authenticity. Disguised depression can be seen as a mid-life slump. Men over the age of forty-five are the new at-risk population for anxiety and depression. Often the dissonance between their authentic self, the self that can form and nurture intimate connections, and their false self, the self that seeks escape from the passion, joy and accountability of intimate connections, becomes unbearable.

Their vulnerability causes a perceived loss of personal power, which can set in motion a cycle of possessive behaviour that is focused on having power or keeping power within their spheres of authority. For family business owners, the family enterprise often becomes the locus of their controlling power. What can go missing

> *"Generativity is the process by which a man ... stop[s] competing so hard and start[s] connecting."*

in action is a sense that real power is developed from within and is derivative of emotional intelligence and self-knowledge. Power is situational and doesn't last forever. However, influence can outlast even our mortal life.

Age-old wisdom regarding mature manhood has always included the notion of selfless generosity, the idea that power and control of ourself and others are at best transitory stages. Classic theories of healthy adult development have concentrated on achieving full autonomy and independence of the self, which is supposed to happen as we separate ourselves from others, particularly our family of origin. But this emphasis is on achieving power and control. Traditionally, little emphasis has been placed on building mutual relationships with mates, friends, coworkers, adult children and community members. These earlier developmental theorists talked about generativity only later in life. Generativity is the process by which a man becomes paternal and creative in a new sense, feeling a voluntary obligation to guide new generations and to mentor younger men and women—in other words, to stop competing so hard and start connecting. This is an important shift for men in the middle stages of life to understand and incorporate, and it is necessary if the relational bank account with their business families is going to bear any fruit.

## Basic Facts About Andropause

### Symptoms of Andropause

- Depression
- Fatigue
- Irritability
- Reduced libido
- Generalized pain
- Sweating and flushing
- Decreased sexual performance—erectile dysfunction

### Short-Term Effects of Andropause

- Decreased strength
- Decreased endurance
- Dermatological changes
- Decreased libido
- Decreased sexual performance
- Feelings of restlessness
- Fatigue
- Loss of self-esteem
- Increased anxiety
- Difficulty concentrating
- Forgetfulness
- Insomnia

### Long-Term Effects of Andropause

- Osteoporosis
- Obesity
- Erectile dysfunction
- Muscle loss

### Diagnosis

Blood test to measure bioavailable testosterone

### Rules For the Road

1. **Give yourself permission to change.** Why fight the inevitable? Be good to yourself.

2. **Move from competing to connecting.** Reconnect with friends. A good barometer for men is to ask, "How many male friends can I count on?"

3. **Develop multiple selves.** To maintain self-esteem and a sense of personal control as you age and change, it helps to foster a variety of passions besides your business. Some men volunteer or take on challenging philanthropic roles. Others learn to play a musical instrument later in life.

4. **Redirect your passions.** Refocus not on the family business you are letting go, but on the new interests that you are pursuing. The key is to maintain passion, because the absence of emotion can depress the immune system.

5. **Let go of maturing children.** Give them your blessing and then spend quality time getting to know them. Many parents vicariously revitalize themselves by learning from their offspring and absorbing the boundless energy of their youth.

6. **Practise perpetual virility.** The most common complaint of married couples today is a lack of sexual desire (usually on the part of the male). And for competitive men running family firms, sex is often number 24 on their to-do list. The key to greater intimacy is a better diet, more exercise and relaxation. But it all starts by talking to your spouse about changes that you are experiencing. Men need to understand that good communication is the key to a long and fulfilling sex life.

# SECTION III

## SUCCESSFUL SUCCESSION:
## HEALING THE PAST,
## ENSURING THE FUTURE

# CHAPTER 10

# OPERATIONALIZING THE GOLDEN RULE

**Golden Rule #1:** *Treat others as you yourself wish to be treated.*
**Golden Rule #2:** *Whoever has the gold makes the rules.*

Transferring power and control from one generation to the next is among the most challenging tasks facing business families. The following tales illustrate the opposite approaches to this undertaking adopted by two business families.

## A Gracious Descent from Power

A father in his late seventies with four children was in the process of transferring some of his last working assets to the next generation. He had already completed a successful transfer of his manufacturing company to one of his sons. (His other three children declined to enter the family business—all were successful and independent professionals.) He had also been working together with his lawyer to transfer the last two-hundred-acre farm to the children. With professional guidance along the way, this business family had developed a fairly sophisticated family council and had established regular family meetings as well as an annual retreat. In anticipation of the father's eightieth birthday I encouraged him to start recording his story and composing his memoirs as a way of preserving his legacy for future offspring.

We gathered at a regularly scheduled family meeting—Dad, Mom and the four children together with a stack of legal documents. The session was lively and productive. Father made a brief speech in which he expressed his wish to transfer his one remaining working asset, namely, his hobby farm, to the children while he was still alive. The adult children asked many questions, seeking and receiving assurances from their parents that this was their genuine desire. With smiles all around, everybody signed the official documents. Then the father asked whether he could table another document to be recorded in the minutes of the meeting. Out of his weather-beaten leather satchel he extracted a sheaf of papers covered with scrawled handwriting that extended from one edge of the page to the other without margins. The lack of margins reflected the frugality of a Depression-era sensibility, which would not allow him to waste paper. He began to read parts of his memoir. It was a typical immigrant story—a rags-to-riches tale of a refugee coming to a new country, paying for his voyage as an indentured farmworker, buying his first piece of land, striking out on an independent venture, and overcoming early struggles involving both failure and success.

For the father, the most important succession issue was the passing on of his legacy and the core values which had created that legacy. This responsibility was more important to him than his wealth, property and working assets. Although his children were familiar with most of the stories, they listened respectfully and more than a few tears were shed. At the conclusion of the meeting the children asked for and received permission from their parents to edit and publish the memoir. As everyone was getting up to leave the meeting, Dad interjected: "Oh, by the way, I have a request. Can I go and buy a new pickup truck for the farm?"

As an outside advisor to this family, I was floored by the simple profundity of this request because gestures of this kind occur so rarely in family business environments. What was so significant about the father's question? He was actually seeking permission from his children. He was asking! Everyone knew that he was wealthy enough to go and buy a new pickup truck at any time. But this father was gracious and intelligent enough to recognize that he had formally passed over control of his farm to the next generation. The story is highly significant because it is so uncommon. If there is one key element to guaranteeing a successful intergenerational succession, it is the graciousness of the senior generation in transferring control and power.

### Sabotaging the Next Generation

Another family handled matters quite differently. A father and one of his sons, Ethan, had worked together on the farm for nearly thirty years. Although the two men had communicated occasionally about future plans, nothing had ever been finalized verbally or on paper. Succession planning became more important to Ethan when, at age forty-five, he was confronted with the return of his own twenty-two-year-old son from agricultural college. The son wanted to discuss and formalize his business relationship within the family farming enterprise. Ethan turned to his father for clarification and codification of their previous verbal understandings and assumptions about a succession plan. Now, however, his sixty-seven-year-old father dug in his heels and refused to discuss the matter any further.

Despite several years of attempts at third-party mediation by close friends and a pastor, the situation went from bad to worse. The father actually pulled out more than two-thirds of the chicken quota in an attempt to undermine his son's ability to farm in a viable manner. Having exhausted all rational forms of intervention, the son, now forty-seven, sought advice about legal recourse. The devastating nature of this intrafamily conflict was producing serious physical symptoms that bordered on a medical crisis for several family members. Adding to the chaos was a lawsuit launched by the father, now seventy years old, against his son. Beyond the exorbitant cost of court proceedings, the cry of "I'll see you in court" represents one of the saddest outcomes for business families and illustrates the tremendous difficulty of and resistance to healthy transfers of control and power.

Three unique issues can sabotage and prevent the orderly transfer of power and control within business families if not handled proactively and creatively.

### Incomplete Grieving

The patriarch of a family business had passed away a number of years ago. Although a memorial service had been held at the time of his death, the family had never conducted an interment service: they had never buried his ashes. For some reason most of the family members who were active in the business continued to be emotionally controlled by their deep attachment to this now-deceased father. Some of that emotional attachment was unhealthy. The family members found it difficult to engage in necessary strategic business planning—or even to get along with each other—because they all had an unresolved connection to the deceased father. Even in death he still controlled most of the family and the family business.

As a way of moving beyond this psychological impasse we scheduled and planned a memorial service together with a pastor who had been a friend of the deceased father and who had conducted the initial memorial service. A new headstone was selected and mounted and a "service of memory" was conducted. This occasion helped many of the family members to experience a healthy grieving process. During the service there was a palpable emotional release for many of the adult children. Afterwards they talked about the cloud that had been lifted and about putting closure to some old wounds. Somehow, through the service, the family was able to move beyond some significant blockages. When incomplete grieving is coupled with strong yet difficult attachments that have not been resolved, the difficulty of transferring control and power increases.

## Family Secrets

Like individuals, families can have secrets that they are ashamed to acknowledge, let alone discuss. Having secrets is not uncommon—we all have them. However, the emotions of shame associated with some secrets and the subsequent inability to talk about them can cause a level of denial and cover-up that is more destructive than the secret itself. The bottom line for business families is that secrets control. Secrets swept under the rug can actually become more powerful over time.

Eventually the "elephant" in the family can become so huge that productive and fruitful communication about other important agendas such as succession planning becomes virtually impossible. For example, some families are unable to acknowledge and name the disease of alcoholism in one of their members. The inability to accept that reality then sets up communication patterns within the family that allow them to deny other realities. If an individual can deny that her brother suffers from alcoholism, then it becomes easier for her to deny that his actions are jeopardizing the viability of the family business or threatening his marriage.

Although our society has become much more sophisticated in terms of understanding the nature of mental illness, it is still all too common to see families circle the wagons in order to deny the existence of mental illness in a vulnerable family member. As with alcoholism, illnesses such as depression, bipolar disorder, addictions and schizophrenia are eminently treatable and also more visible in our culture. However, their presence can still evoke guilt and shame in some families. When the shame associated with feeling inadequate or less than perfect infuses a family system, communication patterns can easily become distorted and we find that the "secret" begins to control the family. By refusing to talk about what is really happening, the family can move into denial and active protection. If the family members can deny something so basic, they can deny anything. One often discovers patterns of denial within families: denial of abuse, denial that the business is facing bankruptcy or that Revenue Canada is threatening. The inability to discuss and talk honestly about what is really happening can be devastating because it does not allow the necessary conversations to occur within the family in order for planning to proceed on the basis of reality. These powerful controlling secrets keep the business family locked up in a rigidly prescribed fantasyland, unable to grow emotionally, relationally and strategically.

### Fear of Change

There is a wonderful quote by Charles Darwin: "It is not the fittest of the species that survive, but the ones that are most capable

> *"It is not the fittest of the species that survive, but the ones that are most capable of change." – Charles Darwin*

of change." Change is a constant in both personal and business environments. It is considered a major source of stress, particularly if the individual's perception of a changing situation engenders fear. Change takes many forms: loss of a loved one, separation from family or spouse, relocation, evolving relationships, health problems, redefined career trajectories, personal growth and workplace shake-ups. For many business owners, retirement signifies massive change, and this change is often the kind that constitutes a major problem, particularly for business owners who derive their primary sense of accomplishment and meaning from owning and managing their business. If I retire, they wonder, will I still be loved, respected and seen as worthwhile by my family, peers and society? Will I still feel good about myself? Will I still be somebody? What will I do with my time? These primal fears constitute the emotional barriers that keep many business owners from engaging in serious succession planning.

No wonder so many business owners unconsciously but rigidly hang on to as much power and control as possible in their businesses. After all, those businesses provide them with a safe and predictable environment which they have created and successfully managed, and therefore they are understandably reluctant to relinquish control only to look into a future abyss which they do not control. At the deepest (and mostly subconscious) level, contemplating succession evokes deep fears of losing control and power in the area that provides their primary identity—namely, their business. So they hang on for dear life. But they do so at the peril of losing both their families and their businesses.

### Signs of Productive Power and Control Transference

In rural communities everyone realizes that the transfer of power and control within a farm operation is going well when they notice that a son is driving Dad's pickup truck around town. On some farms it's the new tractor or combine driven by the next generation that symbolizes successful transfer.

Another significant sign of healthy control transference is the inclusion of next-generation family members at meetings with financial advisors such as accountants and bankers. The authority to sign company cheques is also a clear symbol that the next generation has earned fiduciary trust and that control of financial operations is being shared. Yet another signpost of viable control transference is the involvement of the next generation in the annual budgeting process. In some family businesses positive transference becomes evident when members of the next generation start to organize and lead the annual strategic retreats with senior managers. These ritual moments signal to key staff that true transference of power and control is occurring.

The politics of office space often indicate the level of progress in the intergenerational transference of control. The signs usually begin at the top of the family business food chain. If the founding members are still the first to show up at the office in the morning and the last to leave at night, transference is probably not going well. To allow a succession plan to be effective once agreed upon, it is helpful for the founding generation to take a three-to-six-month extended vacation. This period allows the next generation to cement the loyalty transfer with key staff. Since so much of our identity derives from the spaces we inhabit, some of the most successful succession plans include guarantees that Dad will have a permanent or lifetime office, even if he only shows up for an hour a day or three months of the year.

### Power Problems

### 1. Too Old to Be Parented

Sometimes a father can play his "dad" role inappropriately. In one such example a father reprimanded his son's perceived excess drinking during a business dinner with key clients. The son was in his late thirties and was the CEO of the company. Such treatment is infantilizing, demoralizing and disrespectful to adult children. Even if there are issues or disagreements, parents need to respect next-generation executives and treat them as they would non-family executives. In this case, a private conversation after the dinner would have been more appropriate. When senior family members attempt to exert control inappropriately, they may gain a measure of temporary power, but they lose the long-term ability to truly influence their offspring because such actions engender a loss of respect and credibility.

### 2. Not Listening and Therefore Not Understanding

Many business owners have personalities that err on the side of impatience. The ability to make quick decisions often serves them well in competitive environments. However, the Achilles heel of more aggressive personalities is the lack of "active listening." In one such situation two sons, both vice-presidents, were late for a meeting with senior management. Their father proceeded to give them severe verbal reprimands in front of approximately twenty-five key managers. Although the sons had legitimate reasons for their tardiness, the father did not offer them the courtesy of even a brief hearing, choosing instead to embarrass them in front of peers crucial to the long-term success of the company. This episode festered and created bad blood within the family for months, and I still hear about it years after it occurred. Failure to listen and a rush to judgement are examples of the raw and inappropriate use of power. The long-term result for a business family that is attempting to implement a successful intergenerational transfer of power and control is that the founding parent actually loses influence because his or her advice becomes increasingly irrelevant. The children tune out a father who they feel doesn't really listen or genuinely attempt to understand.

### 3. Undermining Next-Generation Authority

It is often not enough to give next-generation members varying degrees of operational authority. Many long-term key employees will view the new leaders merely as placeholders because they have been conditioned to believe that true power and control resides with the founder. One of the trickier parts of implementing a succession strategy is to effect meaningful loyalty transfers by key staff to next-generation leaders. The companies with the greatest problems are those in which the founders allow staff to bypass the organizational chain of command and gain easy access to them. Permitting this sort of behaviour can make the founders feel momentarily important, but ultimately doing so seriously undermines the ability of the next generation to lead the company into the future. Such patterns are indications of control and power problems for the founders and signal a lack of trust in the next generation. If such incidents occur too often, they severely diminish the effectiveness of a son's or daughter's leadership and can threaten the ongoing viability of the business.

### 4. Inaction on Succession Planning

The most damaging control behaviour is not to do anything—not to plan for succession. During early adulthood (in the thirties) we are driven by the need to plan our own lives and to feel in control of our own futures. By the age of thirty-five, those members of the next generation who want to be involved in the family business have usually committed themselves. However, if they operate for an extended period without a succession plan, they can start to feel trapped or controlled by the inaction of their parents. Chapter 5 presents some statistics on the devastating effects for next-generation family members when succession planning is not handled in a proactive way. The key issue is the perceived lack of control experienced by the younger generation and the disempowering results at both personal and organizational levels.

### What About Power?

Margaret Thatcher, former prime minister of Great Britain, once stated that "being powerful is like being a lady. If you have to tell people you are, you aren't." As one of the most powerful leaders of the twentieth century she drew attention to power as a quality defined by much more than the external trappings of role and position.

An understanding of the proper use of power is essential in business. Unfortunately, some family business leaders serve more appropriately as examples of mismanagement of power, abuse of power and superficial power. When power is exercised in negative ways, business families can be destroyed. Using one's position to squeeze results from the workforce by means of force or coercion can have devastating long-term repercussions because other family members working in the business will quickly find this behaviour oppressive.

Another superficial form of power is built on influence, status and prestige. Younger family members in particular need to recognize that much of their early power in the family business derives from their status as the owners' kids and may have little to do with earned respect. In this case it differs from the kind of power that arises from compassionate and results-oriented abilities. Examples of negative power abound in the case of owner-managers who need to be in charge at all times and can't seem to delegate.

> *"Being powerful is like being a lady. If you have to tell people you are, you aren't."*
> *– Margaret Thatcher*

Such leaders are characterized by an underlying feeling of vulnerability when not in complete control of a situation. Leaders who lack people skills often manipulate their employees, showing disregard for their feelings. Others can be quite insensitive, quick-tempered, irritable and unapproachable—all personality-based negative power traits. Insecurity and low self-esteem can also fuel the need to control people and situations as a way of feeling more self-important. One can summarize the negative use of power by noting that persons who exhibit a high need for control—particularly the need to exercise an inappropriate level of control over others— are usually the most fragile themselves. Their need for control is based on their own misunderstood feelings of fear and the resulting deeper insecurity.

One particular family business leader exhibited a number of these traits, particularly the need to be in charge at all times. He could not rest unless he was micromanaging every detail of his large company. His work consumed him and he regularly put in sixteen-to-eighteen-hour days. His wake-up call came when his marriage began falling apart and he suffered a mini-stroke before the age of forty. With some helpful coaching he realized that micro-managing was not efficient for his business and that some of his natural leadership habits were harmful to both his physical and relational health. The key turning point came when he received intervention and with it insight into the fundamental insecurities driving his dysfunctional "power and control" habits.

Power-oriented behaviour can often mask specific fears or deep insecurity. Real power is rooted in our sense of self-worth and is based on authority that comes from within; people with genuine power have generally earned respect. At our core, most of us experience a struggle between self-acceptance and fear. If fear rules—whether this is a fear of the unknown, fear of failure, fear of exposure or fear of losing control—we will need to control our world, including our business and our family. If there is a sense of acceptance at our core, then our impulse will be to look beyond ourselves and expand our world. People who are grounded in a strong sense of self-worth tend to have more resources with which to serve others. They have more energy for their communities, for serving on boards, for giving to their families and for functioning productively in their occupations or businesses, simply because they are not spending all their energy controlling fears.

People who are fear-based tend to move into what can be called self-protective behaviour. They become overly negative, critical, intimidating, pervasively angry and full of denial. They fantasize, withdraw and shift blame (I'm always right and you're mostly wrong).

Positive power-oriented management emerges when our leadership is based on two complementary sources: relational power and results-oriented power. Relational power comes from an individual's ability to draw people to himself or herself—the ability to earn loyalty because of a genuine interest in relationships. Results-oriented power is the ability to share responsibilities and the ability to work with people to achieve results. Any good leadership development program always involves two grids for evaluating performance. Lasting power comes from the ability to get results as well as the ability to work in productive collaboration with people.

## Negative-Power-Oriented Management Styles

### 1. Power and Approval Seeking

One can overdo the people pleasing, although most approval seekers are seemingly unaware that they are engaged in such behaviour. Nor are they aware that such ingratiating behaviour results in a loss of credibility with the people they are trying to impress.

### 2. Power and Harshly Critical Behaviours

Ridiculing employees' ideas creates a negative work environment. Some leadership personalities, particularly those specializing in quality control, can't seem to escape from their default mode of criticism. Unfortunately, the demoralizing effect on staff stymies creativity and management development within employee ranks.

### 3. Power and the Need to Always Win

Being overtly and relentlessly competitive is usually correlated negatively with effective leadership. Competitive leadership behaviour doesn't give leaders what they really want. Winning is not the same thing as achieving results, and individuals who are running a company want to achieve results. When people are too competitive, someone must always be a loser, and competitive managers lose the synergy and greater long-term results that come from collaboration and teamwork.

### 4. Power and Unquestioned Authority

When managers provide rigid black-and-white answers, their employees become overly dependent and afraid to make any independent decisions. When a business suffers from this type of controlling leadership, momentum and innovation can suffer because the organization retains mostly "Yes" people who lack creativity or are too frightened to challenge their superiors' or the firm's assumptions.

### 5. Power and Judgement

When leaders move quickly to judgement without actively listening, their employees don't feel cared for and sense that they have
little or no control over their work environment. This leadership
style can make it difficult to build significant middle-management
bench strength and retain quality employees.

Power can be exercised in positive or negative ways. Most of us
exhibit a mix of both tendencies. The healthier we are in terms of
our self-confidence and our EQ (emotional intelligence), the better we are able to nurture positive power habits.

### Power and Stress

People who experience the abuse of power and a perceived lack of
control in their personal or working lives can face devastating con-
sequences. The 1997 APEX study is the most comprehensive survey ever done on the ways in which stress affects managers within
the Canadian civil service.[1] It examined more than thirty thousand
upper-management administrators in an attempt to correlate stress
with some key issues. The study found that managers exhibiting significant stress had a 90% greater chance of musculoskeletal problems, a 120% greater chance of cardiovascular diseases, 210% more
instances of gastro-intestinal problems, 350% more coronary disease issues, and a whopping 1740% more mental health disorders!

The biggest revelation of the study was its identification of the
causes of stress for these managers and senior administrators. The
key factor was perceived lack of control. In fact, this was the top
risk factor for all physical and psychological disorders. It was the
largest predictor of health outcomes for senior managers. For all
workplace situations, health risk doubles when individuals do not
have or feel control. If we extrapolate this study into a family business context, it becomes clear why succession planning should be
in place by the time next-generation members are thirty-five. They
need to feel some semblance of control within the business family hothouse.

The APEX study provides a larger context for the difficulties of transferring power and control. It was conducted within the Canadian civil service, but the results can be applied to family business settings. In an October 2006 *Globe and Mail* article, 78% of employers described stress as their top employee health risk concern, yet most had trouble understanding mental health issues and focused the bulk of their wellness initiatives on the promotion of physical health. Only 32% offered stress management programs for employees.[2] This remains a need that employers are slow to recognize and slow to address.

The bottom line is that we could all use more power. We all want more power. Within business families, more power becomes associated with increasing our "circle of love." Having

> **"For all workplace situations, health risk doubles when individuals do not have or feel control."**

more real power, more intrinsic power, actually helps us increase our circle of love. And business families recognize that their circle of love has always been and remains their true competitive advantage.

Recently my wife placed a slip of paper entitled "Truly timeless tips for long-lasting romance" on my desk. This list is a fascinating piece of wisdom coming from an ancient twelfth-century manuscript, and it was surprising to realize how fresh these tips still are. To ensure that the family members in a family business are successful and happy, it helps to make the connection between power and love. Family leaders who truly want to engage the power of their family's "circle of love" need to keep romancing each member. What are some of these twelfth-century tips for romance? Take a look:

### The Power of Romance

- Love is either increasing or decreasing; the love you feel in the early days of a relationship should be only a preview of things to come.
- Intimacy is a work in progress and marriage is an invitation to keep growing closer and closer.
- Just maintaining the status quo is not an option. If your ardour starts to cool you may have to explore new ways to strengthen your connections. Things don't stay the same; ... they either get better or they get worse. If you want to increase the circle of love, get creative.
- Love is always a stranger in the home of greed. Don't be stingy.
- Generosity between lifelong partners is essential in order to stay in love.
- Kindness is not a sign of weakness. Open your hands; open your heart. Remain approachable.
- Winning an argument is a defeat for love. You don't gain anything from having the last word. When your better half loses, you lose too. To resolve a disagreement with your mate, ask more questions. Don't demand explanations. As one good friend keeps reminding me, "Do you want to be right or do you want to be happy?" A lot of us are good at winning battles, but we forget that we are losing the war.
- The faults of the partner are never an excuse to retaliate. If your partner or your children fail you, don't fail them in return. Don't let their infidelity or lies or insensitive behaviour define you. Develop a course of action that is yours and yours alone.

### A Cherokee Tale

One evening an old Cherokee man told his grandson about a battle that goes on inside people. He said, "My son, there is a battle between two wolves. One is evil: it's anger, envy, sorrow, regret, grief, arrogance, self-pity, guilt, resentment, inferiority, lies, false pride, superiority, evil. And the other wolf is good: it's joy, peace, love, hope, serenity, humility, kindness, benevolence, empathy, generosity, compassion and faith." The grandson thought about this for a minute and then he asked his grandfather, "Well, which wolf wins?" The old Cherokee man simply replied, "The one you feed."

We all have choices. What kind of power are we nurturing? We must all find a balance between self-acceptance and ongoing commitment to change those aspects of ourselves that are destructive. As we grow ourselves, our families and our businesses, I trust that some of the insights from this chapter on the difference between negative power and positive power may help to increase that reservoir of relational capital that expands your circle of love.

# CHAPTER 11

# *PRACTISING HABITS OF THE HEART*

*"Sincerity is everything. If you can fake that,*
*you've got it made." –* George Burns

*"Human beings are by nature actors, who cannot become*
*something until first they have pretended to be it. They are*
*therefore to be divided, not into the hypocritical and the*
*sincere, but into the sane, who know they are acting,*
*and the mad, who do not." –* W.H. Auden

*"The weight of this sad time we must obey …*
*Speak what we feel, not what we ought to say."*
– William Shakespeare (*King Lear*)

All humans engage in ritual activity. This is particularly evident during rites of passage such as birth, coming of age, marriage and death. Rituals are extremely powerful because they affect participants inwardly and outwardly at the same time. The performance of meaningful rituals also lies at the core of individual efforts to adapt, survive and grow within family business settings. Family businesses go through predictable patterns of wealth creation, wealth preservation or dissolution, and wealth distribution. Throughout history, successful business families have found ways to celebrate and ritualize the profound meaning that these passages as well as other transitions represent for their members.

The rituals we perform provide pathways for us to follow in our day-to-day activities. Rituals establish order or a sense of what is proper, and they help to create and sustain our communities. Through our rituals we make routine a certain way of seeing, hearing, touching and perceiving our environment. Rituals are also used to restore order. If a custom or law has been breached, as in the case of a theft or a murder, a crisis ensues because society's ritual of self-ordering has failed. Some type of process is needed to address or to redress this situation. Our entire judicial system reflects this notion. Rituals help to define the boundaries of our social interactions. After establishing order, our rituals remind us of the meaning of that established order and help us to maintain that order. When the order is broken, we also have rituals of forgiveness or rituals of legitimation that help restore order.

Children love rituals. If you have children, you have probably observed their desire to watch the same movies over and over again. From the earliest nursery rhymes to the latest picture books, they love repetition. The favourite programs in our home were the *Madeline* series, which my daughters regularly begged me to watch with them. Researchers claim that watching a favourite movie can be beneficial because doing so brings the comfort and deeper understanding that reading a book over and over also provides. Young children have no control over their own lives (for example, when Mommy and Daddy will come home), but a favourite video offers predictability: they know there will be a funny part, that the story will be confusing initially but will become clear, that the ending will make sense of everything. Repeatedly watching a video is their way of mastering and controlling their world. In the same way, the times our daughter spent playing "Dress Up" and "Restaurant" with her friends as a young girl seemed repetitious to us, but this was her way of mastering language, social mores and manners.

As adults we often cling to rituals, particularly during uncertain times. Evan Imber-Black, a family therapist in New York and co-author of *Rituals for Our Times*, states that people "are ritual making creatures" and that "rituals serve the seemingly contradictory functions of providing continuity with the past and of carrying us into the future."[1] We all have family rituals, such as Christmas or

> **"Rituals serve the seemingly contradictory functions of providing continuity with the past and of carrying us into the future."**
> **– Evan Imber-Black**

Thanksgiving, that are well established in the culture. But families also develop their own rituals, such as shared meals, the division of chores, and the manner in which boyfriends and girlfriends are introduced and welcomed into the family.

Rituals help families to maintain closeness, but they can also be sources of conflict. Blended families are particularly vulnerable because of the unfamiliar patterns that new members introduce to the mix. Different practices need to be coordinated when multiple households are involved. In business families, the traditional in-law problem often centres around the integration of a new set of rituals introduced by the in-law. Another problem can occur when families cling to empty rituals, refusing to let go of practices that have lost all meaning. This situation frequently occurs in devout families when older members try to enforce practices such as church attendance on the next generation, even though the adult children may find these rituals boring and meaningless.

### The Magic of Ritual[2]

An informal survey in our community attempted to identify the key factors contributing to longevity in marriage. Using a set of about thirty criteria, participants were asked to select the most important ones and to rank them in terms of their importance in keeping their marriages together. The results were surprising. Predictable factors such as financial stability and a good sex life were not at the top of the list. Instead, the most important factor in marriage longevity—by quite a margin—was the following: whether or not the husband and wife kissed each other goodbye before they went to work in the morning. Interestingly, it didn't seem to matter whether or not they "meant it." What the survey revealed was that a ritual that at first blush seemed superficial carried ongoing meaning for the marriage partners. Just as repeated viewing of favourite movies creates a warm bath of comfort and a

> **"Rituals are habits that establish pathways to emotional intelligence."**

sense of predictability and security for children, so the ritual of a goodbye kiss and embrace seems to provide couples with a habitual anchor in what for many is the unpredictable realm of emotional intimacy.

Why are rituals so effective? The answer lies in their ability to bring together in one event our thoughts, our feelings and our actions. Meaning, emotion and performance merge in an activity that becomes a habit. This ritual habit allows for and can contain often contradictory understandings and feelings in a manageable and predictable pattern. The ritual of dating is perhaps the most common example. It can encompass everything from abject fear of rejection to unbridled lust and passion, all within a cultural matrix of personal responsibility and social accountability. Business families with high emotional intelligence engage in ritual behaviour intentionally and proactively. The following examples demonstrate how family businesses can mine the depth and efficacy of these habits of the heart, individually and communally.

### Rituals of Forgiveness

Marital infidelity, emotional and/or physical abuse, financial or relational betrayal, and disloyalty are among the behaviours and patterns that can destroy families and business partnerships. Too many families have swept pain and heartache under the rug in an attempt to forget the hurt and move on with life. For others, unexamined and unforgiven hurts function as a cancer, eroding and undermining future goodwill.

### A Healing Ritual

A family stuck in the throes of succession planning asked for help in moving beyond certain impasses. After some exploratory interviews and conversations, it became quite evident that a backlog of unresolved hurts and an inability to share the pain openly and honestly were hampering family harmony and business effectiveness. We engaged in a two-step process that we simply called "forgiveness." It began with a ritual of active individual listening and concluded with a group meditation that we called "the ritual of giving and receiving." Implementing the habit of positive active listening is probably one of the most difficult challenges for business families. Although active listening is the essential foundation for all effective communication, it is one of the first practices to fall by the wayside during periods of stress and conflict. In this family it was crucial to develop the skill because some very difficult conversations—most of which would include a very domineering yet fragile father—needed to take place among various groups and individuals.

The active-listening phase took almost a year to complete. However, the important point is that family members began to honestly hear each other and to share some deep-seated feelings of frustration and anger about past events in the family.

We then organized a full-day retreat that included the entire extended family, including in-laws. At the centre of this day-long exercise was a healing ritual that had as its purpose the identification, sharing and healing of emotional baggage within the family. Because some of these emotions were so difficult to locate, let alone express, we used a facilitated process. Blank sheets of paper of various colours were available in the centre of the room—blue, green, red, purple. Participants were invited to write down their feelings according to colour. For example, they could record things they felt sad or depressed about on blue paper. They could express feelings of jealousy on green paper. Red was reserved for anger, and the emotions that energized them could be recorded on purple paper.

A facilitated discussion followed, in which family members were invited to share whatever items they felt comfortable sharing from these different sheets of paper. The exercise may sound somewhat contrived. However, for families that are almost entirely unaccustomed to communicating, let alone communicating about feelings, a programmed ritual exercise such as this one is sometimes necessary to draw out emotions and agendas that could otherwise stay buried for a lifetime. Next, the family members were asked two questions: Which feelings are you willing to let go of? And which feelings do you want to retain? After some personal reflection, participants were given the option of discarding those sheets of paper—and therefore those feelings—that they wanted to release, and we performed a ritual of throwing those discarded sheets into a bonfire.

To conclude this time of healing, family members joined in a meditative exercise of forgiveness. Based on the idea that love is the process of giving and receiving emotional and psychic energy, we asked family participants to focus on two further questions: To whom do you need to express forgiveness? And the corollary question: Where do you need to receive forgiveness today?

Through the rituals of such healing retreats we have seen families achieve new levels of honesty, understanding and intimacy. These breakthroughs were all premised on the capacity to access and communicate feelings in a way that had not seemed previously possible.

We need to recognize that these rituals can provide watershed moments that catapult relationships to new levels. The process of forgiving and healing can take a lifetime, but most of us make the journey along a series of plateaus. Our rituals can provide the impulse to jump-start us to the next plateau. They can also solidify habits that keep us from sliding back down the mountain.

### Rituals of Re-Membering

"People die; relationships don't." On occasion I work with families in which untimely or tragic deaths have occurred. Perhaps a death has taken place recently and the family is still grieving. The emotional intelligence of individuals and families is sorely tested during

> ## "People die; relationships don't."

these times. Since coping with change is difficult even under ideal circumstances and since most of us do not face the experience of losing a loved one on a regular basis, many if not most persons are simply at a loss when dealing with the intense emotions surrounding death.

Feelings of anger, denial, blaming, guilt and (hopefully and eventually) acceptance can all be present. Understanding these feelings and managing them appropriately and constructively can be a challenge. All too frequently—especially if a family member has not had the opportunity or taken the time to grieve—displaced and unresolved anger at the loss of a family member is directed towards other members of the family. Feelings don't simply disappear; free-floating emotions keep on erupting, often unconsciously and too often inappropriately.

After listening to the history of one extended family in which three members died in tragic accidents well before the age of fif-

ty, I realized that many members of this clan had not grieved suffi-
ciently. Intra- and inter-family relations were deeply strained. The
succession planning process was regularly hijacked by personality
conflicts, and inconsequential issues were blown out of proportion.
It had become extremely difficult for some members of the family
to be together in the same room.

The key to handling the impasse within this family business system was the theme of "remembrance." "I remember Uncle Joe …"
"I remember when my wife …" "Remember when our brother
…" The exercise of actively listening uncovered a flood of stories
in which individuals kept referring to their relationships with deceased family members. They were trying to reconnect with important memories and simultaneously attempting to fashion meaningful current family relationships using interpretations shaped by
those memories.

The challenge in such situations is to honour the individual memories despite the many different interpretations that exist
within any family system. Care must also be taken to prevent the
potential grief embedded in those memories from becoming an
additional source of conflict, particularly during times when the
family is negotiating strategic business and estate succession plans.
Individuals and entire families can remain stuck in their attempts
to create a healthy and productive future because of their inability
to deal with the unresolved emotions of a tragic and difficult past.

In this particular situation the family conducted what we called a
"re-membering ritual" or simply a "service of memory." This was a
time for welcoming those members of the family who were no longer present back through the sharing of stories. These stories had
the power to evoke strong memories, all of which were connected
to meaningful feelings. The healing journey proceeded as follows.
The approximately forty living members of the clan were invited to
a potluck and service of memory to be held at their local church on
a Sunday afternoon and evening. Because there was a fair degree
of nervousness and fear about what would take place, it was impor-

tant for the participants to first share a meal together. The nature of the meal—a potluck requiring each individual to bring a dish of some kind—was also important because it allowed all members of the family to participate in the planned activities at that concrete level if in no other way. Everyone brought something to the table, and no contribution was insignificant.

We later regrouped in the church sanctuary, but attempted to keep the service quite informal. Since this family had always been religiously devout, we began with a prayer of receptivity spoken in unison, asking for ease, authenticity and openness to the leading of our hearts as we spoke and listened to each other. We also made

> *"Individuals and entire families can remain stuck in their attempts to create a healthy and productive future because of their inability to deal with the unresolved emotions of a tragic and difficult past."*

the connection between our audible and inaudible voices and the divine presence and we noted that re-membering was a way for the family to maintain vital relationships with deceased kin, even though they were no longer physically present.

Family members were then invited to share stories of departed family members. Many had clearly prepared thoughts and memories that they proceeded to share. After a significant amount of storytelling, the family was led into a time of silent meditation focused on the theme of "light." As brilliantly hued light streamed through beautiful stained-glass panes, participants were asked to silently reflect on how the "light" emanating from the lives and relationships of their departed family members—as experienced personally and as re-membered through the storytelling—felt to them. Furthermore, they were asked to reflect on how re-membering their loved ones could begin to positively influence their actions as they moved into the future. The silence was broken by a prayer of thankfulness for life, for health, for grace, for peace and for the love that existed among them. Finally a petition was made to ask that the light of re-membrance increase the feelings of grace, peace and love among the participants in their current relationships.

After this more formal part of our gathering, the family left the church and walked across the grass to the neighbouring cemetery, where all the deceased family members were buried. In an organic and natural way, individuals proceeded to tell more stories as they stood around the gravesites. Many of them were humorous and quite irreverent. This informal time ended with the family members holding hands in a large circle. Another prayer called upon the spirit of love in all relationships, both past and present, to continue to guide the thoughts and actions of the family going forward. There were many tears. There was much laughter. There was silence. There was fear. There was release. There was new learning and insight. Family members saw each other in new ways and heard each other say things never articulated before. Younger members of the family got a profound history lesson. Older members of the family hoped they would also be thus remembered some day.

This "remembrance ritual" was successful because it provided safe pathways for releasing emotions and thus increased the emotional intelligence of participating individuals and the entire family system. A number of key factors contributed to its positive outcome. Firstly, next-generation members were recruited for the planning committee, and their involvement was strongly cultivated. It was the younger generation, which organized the potluck and helped fashion the service, that provided the necessary momentum and enthusiasm for the event to take place. Interestingly, it was the younger generation that convinced the elders to participate. They were less fearful of this stage of the grieving process. Secondly, the ritual worked because the family had a common religious background and ritual patterns that made our re-membering service more familiar. This helped remove some of the initial uneasiness. Thirdly, the ritual worked because of advance preparation with the "authentic" voices in the family. Any ritual can involve the participation of both authentic and inauthentic voices. The very common criticism, "It's just an empty ritual," reflects patterns of behaving and ceremonies that seem inauthentic.

This healing ritual provided a safe pathway for a family that was starving emotionally because of its inability to grieve. The release of energy for participants that day started a re-patterning in their ways of thinking about and communicating with each other. And that change was embodied in a concrete ceremony, a ceremony that helped them to make sense of the unexplainable—namely, the tragic deaths of persons they loved. Overcoming the fear of death—a step which this ritual allowed and assisted—also helped provide new pathways for overcoming other fears; in this case, the fear of business succession and the changes inherent within that process. Some previously intractable conflicts were overcome and a working succession plan was completed and implemented within a year.

### Ordering Rituals

It is often said that good fences make for good neighbours. In the same way, good family policies make for strong family businesses. Written policies provide guidelines, rules and procedures that form the basis of acceptable ways to do business. Good family policies also provide structured pathways within which to conduct the relationships that are deemed to be the most important for reasons of both kinship and competitive advantage to the family firm. But policies are only effective when they are practised as a rule. Policy binders collecting dust on office bookshelves are usually not worth the paper they are printed on. It is the acquired habits of conduct and procedures practised regularly that make a difference.

Ordering rituals provide a sense of decorum and impose a form of containment on the sometimes unbridled and chaotic patterns of a family business system. Some families seem perpetually locked into conflict patterns that can be quite predictable. Jim knows exactly what to say in order to enrage his sister, and she knows precisely how late to arrive for work in order to irritate her father and yet get her work done. Mother's question about how much the vacation costs sends her married daughter into orbit every time. And the comment about excessive drinking is a sore spot for the youngest son, who has a number of recent DUI charges.

And so the family business merry-go-round continues. Family members have an uncanny ability to probe each other's greatest vulnerabilities and hurt each other. They do not seem to fight fairly. Many family business interactions resemble the squabbling of a group of children in a sandbox.

Given that all persons within a family have vulnerabilities, the attempt to assist families in managing their power relationships requires the practice of ritual containment. The most common containment policy is a family code of conduct. The following example depicts elements that are included in many typical family codes of conduct:

### Code of Conduct

1. No raising of voices.
2. No swearing.
3. No interruptions.
4. Treat others as you want to be treated.
5. No hitting below the belt.
6. Listen for understanding—ask more questions before speaking and judging.
7. You can pass on questions.
8. Fairness rules.
9. Clearly identify and separate the issues under discussion (family, business operations, ownership/estate).

Moving from policy to a functioning code that is regularly practised requires more creative ritualizing. A simple act that can help to instill a code of conduct for business families is to articulate the most cherished values and to write them on a flip chart. Coincidentally, many of our deepest values have their origin in religious traditions. Therefore when family members begin to establish their own codes of conduct, they will often refer to values such as compassion, honesty, respect, love and integrity. These virtues reflect the ideal for most families, and most family members will strive to honour them.

Making the code a habit can be accomplished in playful ways. We have often introduced monetary fines for members of the family who break one of the established rules. For example, in one case anyone who swore was fined ten dollars. The money was placed in a reserve fund that was allocated at the end of the year either to a charitable cause or towards a festivity that everyone participated in.

Two things are important for a code of conduct. The first is the ritual of establishing the code. Codes work best when they are established in a democratic fashion allowing for maximum family participation. The second is to establish rituals of accountability that reinforce the code of conduct on a regular basis. The fines just mentioned are one means of reinforcement. Another is to recite the code of conduct at the beginning of all family meetings. A third very effective way to maintain order is to begin family meetings by formulating and reciting a litany of expectations.

### Transition Rituals

As with policies that never make it out of the policy binder, succession plans that remain confined within accounting documents and legal shareholder agreements do very little to concretely assist the successful transfer of control. Planning and implementing a transition ritual, a formal "passing of the baton" ceremony, can often be extremely important.

In one such situation a father and daughter had finalized a succession plan whereby the daughter would purchase the family business, a Canadian conglomerate operating in four provinces, through a ten-year earn-out. She was also appointed operational president of the company, and the father became chair of the board. The documentation and implementation of all necessary financial and legal documents had been finalized.

On the ground, among the over one thousand employees, the father still commanded incredible loyalty and devotion. It quickly became apparent that although the father had agreed to all of the necessary technical steps required in the transfer strategy, he had no plan to actually relinquish his corner office, nor to change any of his day-to-day work habits. Observing this difficulty, we organized a very formal road show. Father and daughter visited each of their six facilities and spoke with all of the employees in highly scripted town hall meetings—essentially a ritual. Their general "passing the baton" script read as follows:

> **FATHER:** It is my utmost privilege today to make a very important announcement. I have decided to make what is considered in the business world to be the most difficult management decision of my life. I have decided to formally retire from my role as president of this company.
>
> What has given me the confidence to make this decision is that I can hand over the day-to-day reigns to someone who is very capable of managing this company well into the twenty-first century: my daughter Kelly.
>
> Kelly has proven herself in a wide array of management positions in both the public and private sectors. Her academic and professional accomplishments provide her with the necessary tools to drive this business forward in productive ways. Perhaps more important for us is the fact that she has developed a passion for our business that will ensure its ongoing success.

Now, my daughter might not run the business like I have. She might do some things differently. And I want to acknowledge that change is not always easy. But with this passing on of the leadership baton, I want to reassure you that with another R—— at the helm, the values that our family stands for will continue under her leadership.

Kelly, we are very proud of you and promise to support you in this next chapter of R—— Corporation's history.

*(Here the baton was formally passed.)*

**DAUGHTER:** I want to acknowledge that in taking on this new leadership role I am fully conscious that I stand on some pretty big shoulders. My father's genius, creativity and hard work created R—— Corporation. His shoes will be tough to fill.

I realize that I will have a learning curve as I assume full day-to-day responsibility for this company. And I am counting on all of you to assist me in this transitional period of learning.

I also realize that this company is built on the competence and hard work of all its employees and I will always honour your dedication to my father and all of your hard work.

I humbly ask for your support and confidence as we move forward and continue to make this company one we can all be proud of and enjoy coming in to work for each day.

This "passing the baton" ritual accomplished some very profound things. For the father, it drove home the reality of an actual transfer of power and control to the next generation. The content of the scripts, when spoken and listened to repeatedly, began to sink in for both him and his daughter. The ceremony instilled feelings of purpose, worthiness and respect in both participants and allowed them to express thoughts and feelings that they had not expressed or exhibited to each other prior to the road show. The ritual also provided the daughter with a reference point to which she could return for reassurance about her father's sincerity whenever he had difficulty letting go at the office. The ensuing years since the succession strategy was implemented have proceeded quite seamlessly.

## Celebratory Rituals

We all enjoy getting respect. Perhaps no one cherishes it more than a family business owner who has started a business and built it over a lifetime. To be recognized by friends, other business associates and the community at large is a deeply satisfying and memorable experience. To provide that feeling and to recognize the uncommon wisdom and effort that the succession process demands, the Centre for Family Business at the University of Waterloo regularly honours family businesses that have completed a succession process in a meaningful ceremony during its annual spring banquet. This celebration of what is in some ways the ultimate management challenge—succession—includes a number of ritual moments.

Before the event, the Centre assists family businesses in preparing a history of the company, complete with a slide show that involves the taking of many new family pictures. The history is published and also recounted verbally at the spring banquet, and a presentation of the "completed succession" award is made to the family. Members of the family are invited to respond to this honour in front of their peers. The ceremony includes many photo opportunities as well as informal and formal communal recognition. Many of the businesses so honoured proudly display their plaques in the lobby of the corporate office. All parts of this ritual celebratory exercise—the plaque, the ceremony, the preparation for the ceremony and the family interactions during the celebration—reinforce the importance and the profundity of navigating this transition journey successfully.

Some business families celebrate their corporate successes by holding an annual family retreat. The event allows the members of the family—whether active or inactive in the business—to gather for a weekend of recreation, eating, learning and sharing of stories. The entire retreat serves as a ritual time that is both eagerly anticipated and fondly remembered as a moment when the family did something extraordinary and shared quality time.

Within a retreat there are rituals within rituals. New combinations of cousins and siblings play games; different configurations of family members dine together; active and inactive shareholders rub shoulders and find meaningful points of connection not necessarily centred on business activities. In one such retreat we engaged the next generation in an "entrepreneurial simulation" for which the senior generation functioned as adjudicators. This became a very humorous and stimulating way to engage intergenerationally with a key value of this family, namely, the entrepreneurial spirit.

During another retreat I concluded with a Sunday-morning meditation on the topic "Speaker for the Dead." We gave expression to the thoughts and energies of a husband, father, brother and leader of that family business who had died in a recent tragic accident. In giving a voice to someone so beloved and respected, we enabled family members to continue their own healing journey. By synthesizing grief with celebration, corporate meaning with personal purpose, we released positive energy for the next stage in that business family's journey.

> *"We are what we repeatedly do. Excellence, then, is not an act, but a habit." – Aristotle*

# CHAPTER 12

## FROM PARENTING TO PARTNERING

*"I have seen the future and it's a lot like the present, only longer."* – Dan Quisenberry

It was the end of a long and tiring day during an international convention in an industry sector comprised mostly of family business owners. During a panel discussion on succession I was asked the following question: "When should we start preparing our children to take over the family business and how should we go about that task?" I remember quickly responding with two comments. My first was that by the time they reach sixteen we need to have taught our children all the basics necessary for them to be successful later in life, including management of the family business if that becomes their career choice. My second, more flippant comment was, "Try to arrange a marriage for your children before they enter the family business."

As humans we have a biological and social obligation to parent our offspring. As business owners we have a financially driven mandate to manage our employees effectively. In too many business families, parents confuse their roles and end up managing their children and parenting their employees. Ideally we would like to parent and manage equally well. Although it can be difficult to sort out the roles, good parenting sets up good management, and good management allows parenting to remain healthy. Ann Crittenden, in her book *If You've Raised Kids, You Can Manage Anything*, claims that raising children provides parents with the management skills to handle anything.[1] And Barbara Mossberg, president of Goddard

> *"In too many business families, parents confuse their roles and end up managing their children and parenting their employees."*

College, states, "I don't know if one's children can be seen as accomplishments, but certainly I view creating a nurturing structure in which to witness and guide the growth of unique human beings as my most important goal to achieve. I don't take credit for my children, but to me they feel like fabulous accomplishments of my life."[2]

In connecting parenting to managing in this chapter, I make five assumptions: first, that business families view their children and their businesses as being among their greatest assets. Second, that most of us are already good parents, but that in the context of our family businesses we desire to be great parents. Third, we all need to admit that our children can make us look like geniuses sometimes, and conversely that they can humble and shame us. The fourth assumption is that we pick up our parenting style from our "family of origin." Or, to quote a former student and one of my favourite poets, the late great baseball pitcher Dan Quisenberry, "I have seen the future and it's a lot like the present, only longer." The final assumption is that parenting and managing lie on a continuum and that good parenting tends to generate good managers.

The challenge in family businesses is to understand which system we are managing and then to implement clarity and certainty within those boundaries. This is the only way to minimize the confusion between parenting and managing. How do business families balance the loyalty, trust and self-sacrifice that reside in healthy family systems with the need to professionalize management structures based on meritocracy that predominates in successful business environments? We can examine a number of these differences by comparing a set of standard issues within both family systems and business systems.

When it comes to membership, a business family that prioritizes the family over the business will obviously make room for all family members in the business. However, some business families prioritize the business. In that case family members are permitted to join the firm only if they are suitably qualified to do a job that is required and actually available.

Compensation for family members can be tricky. There are two customary approaches to this issue. Family-first business family systems usually err either by paying family members more than the going rate or by underpaying them. In the first case family members become spoiled; in the second, the message being sent is that family members should sacrifice for the "common good." Business-first families determine pay by benchmarking wages to industry standards, which are predicated on the level of responsibility and performance metrics.

Leadership within a family system is often bestowed as a birthright. The oldest son or daughter takes charge or is given authority by virtue of his or her ordinal position. Fathers are given the title of president because they are the oldest male in the family. In a business-first environment, leadership is earned and company officers, whether family members or not, control day-to-day operations.

Resources such as company vehicles, company credit cards, gasoline allowances, cellphones and retained earnings are examples of perks that can be enjoyed by family members within a system that operates under family-first criteria. Within a business-first environment, strategic resources are used exclusively for business purposes and there are firm boundaries between family and business in all financial transactions.

### Family First or Business First?

In family-first environments, outside experience may count for less than the years of service within the family firm when it comes to next-generation advancement. But for business-first family firms, outside experience is often weighted equally to or more heavily than years of service in the family business.

Business families must find a way to balance these family and business priorities. The most successful business families are able to draw clear boundaries between family functions and business operations. They are also able to keep their parenting and management roles separate on a day-to-day basis. One way to envision the difference is to note that most parents strive to treat their children *equally*, whereas in a merit-based business operation managers aim to treat their employees *fairly* by recognizing differences in skills, experience and performance—even among family members. The ability to set boundaries between love and accountability, between equal regard and fair reward, and thus to manage the family business effectively for the long run requires that business owners also parent their offspring for the long run.

### Parenting for the Long Run

According to Jenifer Lippincott and Robin Deutsch, there are three key rules for parenting children well: teach them to stay safe, to show respect, and to keep in touch.[3] I believe that all other parental deliverables derive from these three. If children learn these lessons well, they will be able to translate them into successful careers later. Within the family business or in other career trajectories they will be able to

1. Work ethically and safely within regulatory parameters.
2. Treat everyone, including staff and customers, with respect and dignity.
3. Communicate clearly and accurately.

Teaching these rules of the road is not an automatic process, and learning usually does not happen through osmosis either. There are definite stages to the intergenerational journey from parenting our children to managing family members and eventually to partnering with the next generation.

During the *foundational stage*, we parent in order to keep the ball in play. Continuing with the baseball metaphor, we want to allow our offspring to hit some singles, make some errors and blow some saves. Maybe they will even be sent down to the minors for more seasoning. But they receive constant training and they remain on the team no matter how many times they strike out.

During the *exploratory stage* we parent for power. We expect and/or allow our offspring to hit some home runs. Both parents and children develop scar tissue as we invigorate the performance-management feedback loop.

During the *getting serious* stage we parent for partnership. Controlling each other becomes irrelevant if not destructive. Mutual respect and the complementary influence of partners in dialogue allow the generations to share both the risks and the rewards of operating the family business.

## 1. Foundational Stage: Parenting to Keep the Ball in Play

The foundational stage of parenting extends through the teenage years. A primary concern during this period is to keep our children safe. We teach them about physical safety, how to stay out of trouble and, on a more profound level, we tend to their emotional and/or psychological safety. Some obvious dangers during adolescence include drunk driving, drugs, sexually transmitted diseases (STDs) and unwanted pregnancy. Another primary goal is to teach our children to show respect. The point is not to control their behaviour, but to develop in them the ability to act respectfully towards others and towards themselves. Thirdly, as parents we need to develop in our children the desire and ability to stay in touch with us. We need to know when their plans change and when they are dealing with crisis and we need to be reasonably comfortable with their responses to potentially dangerous situations.[4]

As parents of teenagers we need to remember that *control* over our adolescents is not the point; conversation is. This is probably one of the hardest lessons for parents to master. The sooner we relinquish control, the sooner they can take over responsibility for their actions and decisions. Controlling our children sets up unnecessary communication barriers. Instead, we need to enable their development towards adulthood and independence. Usually the only control required is control over our own temperaments. To acquire this we need to understand our own parenting style and how it impacts our need for control.

**Authoritarian parents** believe that they own the mechanisms of control. In some highly religious families these mechanisms carry the weight of patriarchal domination through a chain of authority coming directly from the divine. Some authoritarian parents dominate their children for other ideological reasons. Many authoritarian styles of parenting are practised unconsciously and derive from the parent's personality and/or unexamined and destructive needs for control. The short- and long-term problem with authoritarian parenting occurs when the parents are not present to micromanage/control their children. Extensive research results demonstrate that the ability to take responsibility for oneself and independent decision-making skills suffer in authoritarian environments.

**Permissive parents** opt to relinquish control and are often so passive that their adolescents are forced to rely on their own inadequate decision-making skills. Too often permissive parenting is actually an abdication of parental responsibilities. That abdication of responsibility can be easily justified by trendy ideological philosophies generally falling under the banner of "allowing children to self-actualize."

**Authoritative parents** communicate a definite point of view to their children. Their offspring gain a clear sense of what constitutes safety; how to define and practise respect; and what it means to communicate regularly and honestly. In other words, authoritative parents manage the mechanisms of control without micromanaging their children's every move. Authoritative parents are skilled at delineating acceptable boundaries, managing channels of power, and communicating actively in order to achieve long-term influence.

The foundational stage of parenting is probably the most difficult and also the most important. Unless families achieve a certain level of success at this stage, it becomes increasingly difficult to pursue further stages of intergenerational partnering in a family business. To put the point another way, the chances of effecting a smooth and successful family business transition diminish significantly if this foundational stage is not navigated well.

### Foundational Signposts

Six signposts mark progress during the foundational stage. Initially, much of our foundational parenting involves helping children achieve success at school and competence in educationally related activities. School remains the dominant early context within which children begin to master tasks, information and skill sets. Within the limits of our children's capacities, our foundational parental challenge is to assist them in achieving acceptable levels of success in school and to master developmentally appropriate learning goals.

A second foundational signpost involves the socialization process of our children. Are they good team players? Can they function productively in a group setting, whether on a sports team or on the line in the family shop? What is their capacity to establish and maintain friendships?

A third foundational indicator involves their ability to take initiative. Are they self-motivated? Do they get themselves up in the morning to attend school or go to work on time? Do they view life as a challenge to embrace with energy or are they passive consumers of info-entertainment?

Fourthly, the healthy self-esteem of our children is probably the ultimate goal of all our parental activities and the foundational pre-requisite for their subsequent maturation and growth. Developing self-esteem and self-confidence is a particularly difficult challenge for teenagers, whether it pertains to peer pressure and social accep-tance, body image and self-regard, sexual identity or healthy sexu-al expression.

A fifth signpost involves accountability with money. Next to sex, money is the most difficult topic for families to discuss. Yet our children need to receive an early dose of reality and awareness about finances, including how to balance a cheque-book, saving, spending, tithing, the relationship of risk to re-ward, compound interest and rudimentary investment advice. Without this early understanding they will find it much more difficult to achieve later financial independence, fiscal responsi-bility and sound fiduciary decision-making skills when involved in the family business.

The sixth foundational signpost pertains to character develop-ment and is identified by two behavioural characteristics: kind-ness and humility. A great deal of current leadership research (notably *Good to Great*, a landmark book by Jim Collins[5]) has es-tablished that top leaders demonstrate a compelling modesty, are rarely boastful, are generous in handing out praise and are calm-ly but clearly achievement-oriented without necessarily being ag-gressively competitive.

When we summarize the signposts that mark the foundational stage of parenting, we find that the list echoes the patterns iden-tified by Collins in *Good to Great*. The great companies achieved breakthroughs that allowed them to surpass the merely good firms by developing disciplined people, engaging in disciplined thought and then moving toward disciplined action. Our funda-mental task as parents is to launch our children down the road of thinking and behaving with the discipline inherent in the six foundational signposts:

1. Success and competence in school.
2. Good team spirit.
3. Self-motivation.
4. Self-esteem.
5. Money accountability.
6. Kindness and humility.

## 2. Exploratory Stage: Parenting for Power

The exploratory stage covers the years from roughly twenty to thirty. During this time parents/coaches explore the availability and readiness of their bench strength as their firm gets ready for either spring training, a mid-season correction, or perhaps a pennant drive. As they assess their team needs, they might be looking for a utility infielder, a clean-up hitter, a starting pitcher, a catcher who can quarterback the team, or perhaps even a new manager. As they look down the family roster, they as parents and bosses might see only a group of kids barely out of college with varying levels of experience and with no discernible sense of direction or passion. As discussed earlier, this stage is ripe for disaster unless parents/bosses observe some intentionality in separating their two disparate roles. Perhaps "coaching" describes the most effective style of working with the next generation during this mutual exploration of career options.

Again, six signposts characterize this parenting-for-power exploratory stage. Although parental authority and power wane significantly during this period as the next generation emerges into adulthood, I believe there is one signpost, related to the type of work experience required for a long-term career in the family firm, that parents/coaches need to insist upon. Best practices would indicate that next-generation members make the best career decisions and end up being most productive within the family business if they have at least three to five years of solid work experience outside the firm. That external experience, coupled with a deliberate rotation through a variety of jobs within the family business, provides the necessary experiential basis for both generations to complete their due diligence concerning future partnership.

Secondly, if owners/coaches want their children to seriously consider joining the family business, they have an obligation to clarify

> *"Best practices would indicate that next-generation members ... end up being most productive within the family business if they have at least three to five years of solid work experience outside the firm."*

their mission and their business philosophy. Why does the family business exist? What is its unique purpose? What are the underlying values and assumptions informing the way it currently operates and the way they wish it to operate in the future? Next-generation members deserve to know and understand the type of business environment to which they are considering committing the rest of their professional life.

Professionalization characterizes the third exploratory signpost. Establishing company-wide criteria and policies for hiring, remuneration, performance reviews and promotions removes the perceived arbitrary nature of many parent-child relationships within business contexts. The onus is on the current business owners to establish these professional guidelines and policies, to communicate them clearly and often, and to implement them rigorously and fairly. This manner of operating is essential to any well-managed company. However, in a family-owned and -managed operation, the extra level of professionalization inherent in well-established policies and procedures prevents high emotions, family biases and perceived arbitrariness from skewing healthy decision-making during the exploratory process.

For anyone seriously considering the elevation of one or more next-generation members to leadership roles, I would strongly encourage a fourth signpost, the involvement of a mentor. Whether this mentor is an executive coach, a trusted senior manager of the business, an industry expert or a wise counsellor, he or she should come from outside the family. A neutral external advisor can provide helpful career counselling and can provide the next generation with a safety valve when potentially difficult family dynamics need to be processed.

Fifthly, during the exploratory period, families cannot afford to neglect the building of relational capital. Sometimes in our hurry to elicit a decision from our children regarding their future in our business, we forget that no matter what the final career decision, we will still remain a family. Parenting during this phase needs to intentionally capitalize on family relationships, on enjoying each other as friends and not just as business colleagues. One way to accelerate the growth of intentional relational capital is for parents to organize an annual family retreat with a focus on celebration, leisure activities and intergenerational shared laughter rather than on business issues. Since the exploratory years are perhaps the most difficult ones to navigate for both parents and their emerging adult children, building shared positive experiences helps ensure adequate relational capital in the family. This becomes essential to future collaboration and partnership in the family business.

The sixth exploratory signpost involves job-shadowing and performance evaluations. During the exploratory phase, adult children who are interested and/or working in the business need to be invited to key business meetings, including those with suppliers, customers, bankers and shareholders. Not only does this provide them with a more realistic understanding of the larger parameters of the family business, but it also helps them plan their own career trajectory within the business. As they sort out what they enjoy doing and what they think they are good at doing, it becomes imperative near the end of the exploratory stage to engage them systematically in brutally honest performance-feedback and leadership assessments. Most people do not achieve their best work performance until their mid-thirties. Given this fact, it is crucial that owners/parents find ways to "grow the next generation" through the use of accurate performance assessments and regular and honest evaluation.

Remember, during this stage the main goal of parents is to coach their children so that they will develop the personal power to make genuine decisions, whether or not they wish to enter the family business.

### 3. The "Getting Serious" Stage: Parenting for Partnership

The "getting serious" stage optimally occurs before the next generation turns forty. I have seen some next-generation members move into partnerships with their parents during their twenties and others do so in their fifties. However, as adult children enter their forties, their drive for autonomy and control over their own lives and future begins to exacerbate difficulties within family firms that have not engaged in serious succession planning. Transitions are always a dance and there is no one optimal way to accomplish an intergenerational succession. However, there are signposts for success. Getting serious about succession requires that senior family members parent their children as if they want them to become business partners. It requires that they "bless" their sons or daughters by communicating some version of the following message:

> *I look forward to becoming your business partner with the understanding that we are transitioning financial and operational control of the family business into your capable hands over the next (——) years. I trust your commitment, I am confident in your abilities, and during this transition I want to assist you in every way possible to make this company even more successful than it is today.*

If an owner/parent cannot honestly repeat some version of this blessing to family members contemplating succession, then he or she has other compatibility problems requiring serious attention.

The signposts for the "getting serious" stage all begin and end with trust. Trust is what family relationships are about. Trust is what makes human organizations possible. Trust is the real glue in every deal. Trust operates at three levels simultaneously. Family members usually trust each other to be fundamentally honest. Committed partners exhibit a deeper level of trust, one that includes shared motives and goals. They trust that the other partner won't hurt them and that he or she has their best interests at heart. And family business partners trust each other's competence. In other words, each family member trusts the other to do a good job in a situation whose outcome will significantly affect both. If just one of these levels of trust is not present, its absence quickly erodes the others, and soon the business family can find itself operating in a very low-trust environment.

## The Impact of Trust and Mistrust

| High-Trust Environments | Low-Trust Environments |
| --- | --- |
| • Feelings of comfort and safety | • Feelings of anxiety and insecurity |
| • A culture of fairness | • Misuse of power |
| • Optimism about the future | • Uncertainty about the future |
| • Loyalty and commitment | • Eroding loyalty and commitment |
| • Vision of the common good | • Self-interest/personal agenda |
| • Increased motivation | • Decreased motivation |
| • More effective communication | • Less sharing, listening, openness |
| • Higher productivity | • Lower productivity |
| • Ownership and accountability | • Self-protection and blaming |
| • Spirit of cooperation and respect | • Unhealthy competition |
| • Higher-quality relationships | • Increased conflict |

In the kind of high-trust environment necessary to consummate family business succession decisions, the following characteristics are evident. Members feel very secure. Instead of misuse of power, a culture of fairness predominates. There is optimism about the future. Employees and shareholders exhibit loyalty and commitment. Everyone shares a vision of the common good. Family members and employees demonstrate increased motivation. Effective communication takes place and an atmosphere of listening and openness pervades the shop. Productivity is high. People take ownership of decisions and results and exhibit a high degree of accountability for all aspects of the business. A spirit of cooperation and respect governs teamwork. And generally higher-quality relationships prevent disagreements from becoming major conflicts.

Another key signal that the next generation is serious about partnering in the family business occurs when younger family members are ready and willing to put some "skin in the game." In other words, they are willing to invest some of their own risk capital. Perhaps the young next-generation member refinances his house and puts a thirty-thousand-dollar down payment on the purchase of the business; the amount matters less than the principle of having some shared risk in the venture. The greatest succession successes occur when generational partners share sweat equity and financial risk. Now we are talking *serious*.

## A Warning on the Use of Trusts

One of the most common questions I am asked concerns the use of trusts for business families contemplating business succession and estate planning. My first response is to proceed with caution. Simply put, trusts are used when you don't trust or have confidence in someone or some future situation. Within family firms, trusts often serve as stark legal reminders that the senior generation (trustees) controls the next generation (beneficiaries). This might be necessary when members of the next generation are quite young or if there are vulnerable members of the family in need of fiduciary oversight. But trusts can become problematic when used indiscriminately with adult children. Notwithstanding that caution, the use of trusts in transition planning is widespread and can provide elegant technical solutions to a variety of important issues. Foremost among them, trusts help to minimize taxes and protect assets from potential creditors.

But the knee-jerk and less-than-thoughtful application of trusts during family business transitions often undermines precisely the trust and loyalty that should form the core competitive advantage of business families in the first place.

Trusts can stunt the development of the next generation. By definition, the beneficiary of a trust is passive and the trustee(s) are responsible for protecting the beneficiaries. In one case, the deceased parent's attorney and accountant had the responsibility to vote the shares of all three siblings. Although these siblings were now in their thirties and forties, they could not take responsibility for providing strategic direction to the family business that constituted their major asset.

Of course one assumes that trustees appointed by the parents will act in responsible—generally translated as "conservative"—ways. Often the real problem with overuse of trusts is that it leaves the next generation as passive shareholders and undermines their growth into responsible directors who can make informed and appropriate governance decisions. And it can leave the next generation with the mistaken conclusion that all succession issues have been taken care of. Business succession planning is not the responsibility of trusts. Trusts function as one among many estate planning tools.

# CHAPTER 13

## *TOWARD VITAL BUSINESS FAMILIES*

> *"A family is vital to the extent that it energizes and nurtures the abilities and talents of both children and their parents. What distinguishes the vital family is its emphasis on lifespan human development, its recognition that both children and adults undergo continuous change and growth, and its adaptive melding of unilateral and mutual authority."* – David Elkind[1]

Most family firms function legally as corporations. According to Webster a corporation is "a body formed and authorized by law to act as a single person although constituted by one or more persons and legally endowed with various rights and duties including the capacity of succession."[2] Any self-respecting lawyer would counsel families engaged in economic activity to incorporate in order to limit legal liability. Most accountants also encourage incorporation in order to maximize tax efficiencies within existing national tax revenue regulations. Thus, economists would generally regard the "family corporation" as a functionally defined productive enterprise.

However, the family firms that seem to be most successful in balancing their complex set of goals and effecting orderly succession strategies often operate under a much broader understanding of incorporation. Although seldom articulated and often carried out unconsciously, the practice of such successful family firms embodies a deeper sense that "incorporation is a concession of public authority to a private group in return for service to the public good, with effective public accountability."[3] Such a beneficent role for family companies indicates a shift from a purely legal definition of the corporation as a profit-generating and profit-maximizing institution to one defined in political and religious-social terms. Many successful business families demonstrate the extent to which furthering the common good in economic matters can function as a not-so-secret strength for positioning their companies in local, regional and international marketplaces. Furthering the common good or "practising enduring habits of the heart" also defines them internally, as family members attempt to partner around a shared vision of common values and goals.

The noted child psychologist David Elkind wrote the following in his 1994 book *Ties That Stress: The New Family Imbalance:*

> A family is vital to the extent that it energizes and nurtures the abilities and talents of both children and their parents. What distinguishes the vital family is its emphasis on lifespan human development, its recognition that both children and adults undergo continuous change and growth, and its adaptive melding of unilateral and mutual authority.

Elkind's book identifies the building of relational capital as essential to the success of family firms. The depth of relational capital determines the vitality of a family. Vital families require the input of hard work and energy. Creating and sustaining vital families thus becomes an essential adult responsibility. It is only when we as adults move beyond self-interest and partner with the next generation out of a genuine commitment to their future well-being that we demonstrate a sense of generativity. And it is this intergenerational flow of relational capital which characterizes our essential legacy.

M. Scott Peck's book *The Road Less Travelled*, which also advocates the benefits of investing energy in order to make relationships work, argues that relational capital is not a gift from heaven, nor can it be arranged through a contract.[4] Relational capital is built by consistent efforts to confront and resolve differences, to communicate openly, and to accept and support one another's continuing growth and development. The long-term health of family businesses depends on families with this kind of vitality.

Most business families share a genuine modesty regarding their business success. Nevertheless, many of the other key habits of successful family businesses described in this book would not be as effective in the absence of a family culture of ethical integrity and philanthropy. In an age characterized by both excessive corporate greed and remarkable corporate social responsibility, family firms continue to lead by example, informed by family values deeply nurtured within their respective circles of love and caring.

# APPENDIX 1

# SUCCESSION PLANNING TEMPLATE

### Stage 1: EXPLORATION

a. Determine the facts of the situation (relational, financial, operational).
b. Clarify objectives of all stakeholders within each circle (family, operations, ownership).

### Stage 2: DIAGNOSIS

a. Assess relational, financial, operational strengths and challenges.
b. Measure professional partnership capacity.

### Stage 3: INTERVENTION/INSTRUCTION

a. Facilitate difficult conversations.
b. Explore creative solutions.
c. Negotiate a go-forward strategy.

### Stage 4: IMPLEMENTATION

a. Strategic business plan.
b. Contingency plan.
c. Leadership succession plan.
d. Ownership succession plan.
e. Founders' retirement plan.
f. Shareholder agreement(s).
g. Estate plan.
h. Next-generation development plan.

# APPENDIX 2

## FOR PROFESSIONAL ADVISORS

### The Anatomy of a Succession Planning Engagement

Not all professional advisors feel comfortable integrating the soft issues or family agenda during the succession planning process. Yet professionals who must facilitate results through regular client meetings, through group work, and particularly within emotion-driven family-based systems will hopefully find this book instructive. After reading and incorporating the key insights of *The Family Business Doctor* you will learn to do the following:

### 1. Understand Family Business Dynamics

Familiarizing yourself with the family business cases discussed in this book will provide you with knowledge about the interdependent dynamics of family and business systems. You will gain a deeper appreciation for the high-octane power within family business environments and will learn not to fear the challenging emotional settings of this specialized field.

### 2. Identify the "Red Flags" During Family Business Succession

Identifying and discussing the "red flags" buried in technical documents such as shareholder agreements, estate freezes, wills and trusts, etc., is sometimes very difficult for more technically oriented advisors. This book will help you identify those hidden land mines more quickly and go beyond technical jargon in order to assist your clients in understanding and effectively communicating about the more personal and emotional issues they might raise.

### 3. Use and Adapt Effective Roadmaps for Family Business Settings

This book introduces you to a variety of assessment and intervention tools and strategies adapted from the fields of human development and organizational behaviour that can be applied to working with your family business clients.

## Concluding Tips

1. *Determine whether you are functioning as an "expert advisor" or as the "trusted quarterback."* Some situations require a full psychological assessment, or a forensic financial audit, or a comprehensive shareholder agreement, or an estate freeze, or a retirement financial plan. These are time-specific and well-defined surgical procedures. The longer-term role of shepherding the exploratory, diagnostic and intervention phases of a complex and often emotion-laden business family transition plan requires either the services of an interdisciplinary team or a multi-disciplinary professional with significant background in behavioural and human development.

2. *Follow the "Hippocratic oath"—above all else do no harm.* As professionals we need to fully understand when we are out of our personal comfort zone and more importantly out of our professional depth.

3. Starting with implementation strategies before a full exploration of all the facts and a comprehensive diagnostic assessment is tantamount to prescribing an aspirin for a brain tumour. Best practices research and experience provides the compelling logic to *follow the succession planning template as outlined.*

4. Remember that the average succession planning process takes two to five years to complete. *Succession planning is one long communication exercise.* Lay the foundation for better communication pat-

terns early in that process by identifying dominant functional and dysfunctional communication patterns within the family.

## Our Most Important Contributions

**Keep hope alive:** Too many business families seem paralyzed by inaction, aware that things have to change in order to preserve and enhance family relationships, yet handcuffed even further by the fear of change. We need to encourage, to strengthen resolve, to provide hopeful stories of success. If we as advisors can keep instilling hope, then individuals and their families can often chart a course leading to ultimate success.

**Normalize anxiety:** Most families need reassurance that they are not crazy or totally dysfunctional. Every family is dysfunctional in its own unique way, and this book helps our clients identify the unique and completely common issues residing in most business families. We help reduce anxiety by predicting situations and outcomes and injecting humour.

**Mirror reality:** To be effective we do need to expose fantasies—within all generations. Good advisors keep holding up a mirror to the individuals within the family and to the family system as a whole in order to reality-check their assumptions. And we must speak the truth in a compassionate manner.

**Think creatively:** One of our primary tasks is to keep families from getting locked into a plan too early. A too-rigid defence of one particular option will usually result in a succession plan that won't stand the test of time. Solutions have to be win-win if family health and harmony are to prosper and survive. And they can't be our pre-determined solutions. Our primary task as advisors is to help our clients think better—with clearer focus, with more courage, and with a deeper understanding of all the facts.

**Inject best practices:** As advisors, we bring a well-developed "body of knowledge" to bear upon a once-in-a-lifetime succession management challenge for family business owners. We must be familiar with that repository of expertise and willing to share it generously and appropriately.

# NOTES

### CHAPTER 1. THE COMPETITIVE ADVANTAGES OF FAMILY FIRMS

1. Leslie Brokaw, "Why Family Businesses are Best," *Inc.*, March 1992, 73–81.
2. Gordon Pitts, *In the Blood: Battles to Succeed in Canada's Family Businesses* (Toronto: Doubleday Canada, 2000).
3. Adam Bellow, *In Praise of Nepotism: A History of Family Enterprise from King David to George W. Bush* (New York: Doubleday, 2004).
4. Joseph Weber et al., "Family, Inc.," special issue, *BusinessWeek*, November 10, 2003.
5. Ronald C. Anderson and David M. Reeb, "Founding-Family Ownership and Firm Performance: Evidence from the S&P 500," *Fortune*, June 2003, 1301–1327.
6. Philippe Tibi, as quoted in *Financial Times*, October 25, 2003.
7. Adam Hanft, "Mom & Pop: Please Read," *Inc.*, September 2003.

### CHAPTER 2. THE FOUR UNIQUE CHALLENGES FACING BUSINESS FAMILIES

1. *The BDO Dunwoody/COMPAS Report on Canadian Family Business—Summary* (Toronto: BDO Dunwoody/COMPAS, 2003), 4.
2. *American Family Business Survey* (Springfield, Mass.: MassMutual Financial Group/Raymond Institute, 2003).
3. *Are Canadian Family Businesses an Endangered Species? The First Success Readiness Survey of Canadian Family-Owned Business* (Waterloo, Ont.: Deloitte & Touche/ University of Waterloo School of Accountancy, 1999).
4. *The BDO Dunwoody/COMPAS Report on Canadian Family Business* (Toronto: BDO Dunwoody/COMPAS, 2003).

### CHAPTER 3. THE PRIORITY OF A COMMON FAMILY VISION

1. Stephen R. Covey and Sandra Merrill Covey, *The Seven Habits of Highly Effective Families* (New York: Simon & Schuster Ltd., 1999), 9.
2. F. Walsh, "Healthy Family Functioning," *Family Business Review* 7 (June 1994): 175-198.
3. Covey and Covey, *The Seven Habits of Highly Effective Families*.

### CHAPTER 5. THE VULNERABILITY OF THE NEXT GENERATION

1. Gail Sheehy, *Passages: Predictable Crises of Adult Life* (New York: Bantam Dell Doubleday Publishing Group, 1974).
2. J.A. Davis and R. Tagiuri, "The Influence of Life Stage on Father-Son Work Relationships in Family Companies," *Family Business Review* 2 (March 1989): 47–74.
3. David Bork, *Family Business, Risky Business: How to Make It Work* (Aspen, Colo.: Bork Institute for Family Business, 1993).

## CHAPTER 6. COMMUNICATING WITH EMOTIONAL INTELLIGENCE

1. Daniel Goleman, Annie McKee, and Richard E. Boyatzis, *Primal Leadership: Realizing the Power of Emotional Intelligence* (Boston: Harvard Business School Press, 2002).
2. Peter Salovey and Marc A. Brackett, *Emotional Intelligence: Key Readings on the Mayer and Salovey Model* (Port Chester, N.Y.: Dude Publishing, 2004).
3. Reuven Bar-On and James D.A. Parker, eds., *The Handbook of Emotional Intelligence: Theory, Development, Assessment, and Application at Home, School and in the Workplace* (San Francisco, Calif.: Jossey-Bass, 2000).
4. Daniel Goleman, *Emotional Intelligence: Why It Can Matter More than IQ* (New York: Bantam Books, 2006).
5. Richard Boyatzis, Elizabeth Stubbs, and Scott Taylor, "Learning Cognitive and Emotional Intelligence Competencies Through Graduate Management Education," *Academy of Management Learning and Education* 1, no. 2 (2002): 150–162.
6. R.F. Baumeister, "The Psychology of Irrationality: Why People Make Foolish, Self-Defeating Choices," in *The Psychology of Economic Decision*, vol. 1, *Rationality and Well-Being*, ed. Isabelle Brocas and Juan D. Carrillo (Oxford: Oxford University Press, 2003).

## CHAPTER 7. "FOUNDERITIS" AND THE CHALLENGE OF HEALTHY AGING

1. Norman Doidge, *The Brain that Changes Itself: Stories of Personal Triumph from the Frontiers of Brain Science* (New York: Viking Penguin, 2007), xvi.
2. H.C. Lehman and D.K. Simonton, *Late Life Potential*, ed. M. Perlmutter (Washington, D.C.: Gerontological Society of America, 1990), 103.
3. Gene D. Cohen, *Uniting the Heart and Mind: Human Development in the Second Half of Life* (San Francisco, Calif.: American Society on Aging, 2004).

## CHAPTER 8. SOBs (SONS OF BOSSES)

1. John Thies and Peter Naus, "The Importance of His Father's Blessing to a Man's Sexuality," *The Canadian Journal of Human Sexuality* 1, no. 3 (1992): 147–154.
2. Neil N. Koenig, *You Can't Fire Me, I'm Your Father: What Every Family Business Needs to Know for Success* (Washington, D.C.: Kiplinger, 2000).
3. John Updike, *Rabbit is Rich* (Toronto, Ont.: Random House, 1981); John Updike, *Rabbit at Rest* (Toronto, Ont.: Random House, 1990).

## CHAPTER 9. MALE MENOPAUSE: THE HIDDEN FEAR

1. William J. Cromie, "Marriage Lowers Testosterone: Hormones Range Less on the Homestead," *Harvard Gazette*, September 19, 2002.
2. Ibid.
3. Gail Sheehy, *Understanding Men's Passages* (Toronto: Random House, 1998).
4. Ibid., 42.

## CHAPTER 10. OPERATIONALIZING THE GOLDEN RULE

1. *Work Habits, Working Conditions and the Health Status of the Executive Cadre in the Public Service of Canada* (Ottawa, Ont.: Association of Professional Executives of the Public Service of Canada, 1997).

2. Virginia Galt, "Employers Cite Stress as Top Health Risk," *The Globe and Mail*, October 27, 2006.

## CHAPTER 11. PRACTISING HABITS OF THE HEART

1. Evan Imber-Black and Janine Roberts, *Rituals for Our Times: Celebrating, Healing and Changing Our Lives and Relationships* (Toronto, Ont.: Random House, 1998).

2. Tom F. Driver, *The Magic of Ritual: Our Need for Liberating Rites That Transform Our Lives and Our Communities* (New York: Harper Collins, 1991).

## CHAPTER 12. FROM PARENTING TO PARTNERING

1. Anne Crittenden, *If You've Raised Kids, You Can Manage Anything: Leadership Begins at Home* (Toronto, Ont.: Penguin, 2004).

2. ———, "Time to Put Motherhood on Your Resume," *The Globe and Mail*, March 25, 2005.

3. Jenifer Lippincott and Robin Deutsch, *Seven Things Your Teenager Won't Tell You and How to Talk to Them Anyway* (New York: Random House, 2005).

4. Ibid., 10ff.

5. Jim Collins, *Good to Great: Why Some Companies Make the Leap and Others Don't* (New York: Harper Collins, 2001).

## CHAPTER 13. VITAL FAMILIES EQUAL HEALTHY BUSINESSES

1. David Elkind, *Ties That Stress: The New Family Imbalance* (Boston: Harvard University Press, 1994).

2. *Merriam-Webster's Collegiate Dictionary*, 10th ed., s.v. "Corporation."

3. Robert N. Bellah, *Habits of the Heart: Individualism and Commitment in American Life* (Los Angeles: University of California Press, 1996), 290.

4. M. Scott Peck, *The Road Less Travelled* (New York: Touchstone, 1978).

# ABOUT THE AUTHOR

**Dr. John Fast** is the founder of the Centre For Family Business, affiliated with the University of Waterloo and serving southwestern Ontario. It was the first such centre in Canada and is now considered one of the largest in North America. He has co-authored numerous books and curriculum used by professionals and family firms, including the *Agri-Succession Case Study Commentary*, published by the Canadian Farm Business Management Council. John brings a background as counsellor, entrepreneur, ethicist and educator to bear upon a successful career coaching executives and leading organizations through transitional dynamics. As an active researcher and speaker, he addresses numerous trade, professional and academic audiences each year. John is a sought-after inspirational speaker on topics related to family business, retirement, work-life balance, leadership, and workplace integrity. He is currently the founding partner and president of Family Enterprise Solutions, a management consulting and training organization through which he has emerged as one of Canada's leading experts on family business. His forthcoming book, *The Family Business Doctor*, has received wide acclaim for its ability to communicate the deepest issues facing business families in a hopeful and constructive manner.

# ADDITIONAL INFORMATION

If you found this book thought-provoking …
If this book has inspired you …
If you are interested in having Dr. John Fast speak to your organization or design a workshop or seminar for your company, family, school or team …

**Contact us for a complete list of topics or visit:**

John Fast
Family Enterprise Solutions
266 Stanley Drive
Waterloo, Ontario
Canada
N2L 1J1

Email: johnfast@familybusinessdoctor.ca
Website: www.familybusinessdoctor.ca